CW00725039

Good Fell⟨

—— *of* ——

PADSTOW

For Rosanna and family will every good

by

BARRY KINSMEN

Barry Kinsmen

Published by

𝔗𝔥𝔢 𝔉𝔢𝔡𝔢𝔯𝔞𝔱𝔦𝔬𝔫 𝔬𝔣 𝔒𝔩𝔡 ℭ𝔬𝔯𝔫𝔴𝔞𝔩𝔩 𝔖𝔬𝔠𝔦𝔢𝔱𝔦𝔢𝔰

GOOD FELLOWSHIP OF PADSTOW

© Copyright 1997 Barry Kinsmen

ISBN 0902660276

Published by the Federation of Old Cornwall Societies

All rights reserved. This book is protected by copyright.
No part of it may be reproduced, stored in a retrieval system,
or transmitted in any form or by any means electronic, mechanical,
photocopying, recording or otherwise without written
permission of the publisher

Designed & Printed
by
d P e A s R i K g E n R s
35 Lodge Hill, St. Blazey Gate, Par, Cornwall

DEDICATION
To the 'Good Fellowship of Padstow' and its people

BIOGRAPHICAL DETAILS

Barry Kinsmen was born at Hawkers Cove in Padstow. He was educated at Padstow C.P. School and Bodmin Grammar School. His great love of history was engendered in those years. He was formerly Headteacher of St. Issey School and later Rector of St. Issey and St. Petroc Minor (Little Petherick) and Diocesan R.E. Adviser. He was Town Mayor of Padstow in 1974-75.

In 1977 he became a Bard of the Cornish Gorsedd, taking as his bardic name 'Bugel Petrok'.

Now living in retirement in Padstow, he is currently Chairman of Padstow Old Cornwall Society.

His many interests include local history, reading, walking, music, 'the weather' and people.

TABLE OF CONTENTS

ACKNOWLEDGEMENTS

I would like to extend my grateful thanks to everyone who have encouraged me and supplied information and support to me in writing this book.

To members of my family especially cousin Jill who typed the original manuscript.

To the artist Mary H. Grierson for allowing me to use her painting on the front cover.

To the executive committee of the Federation of Old Cornwall Societies and their publications officer Robert Evans for publishing this account of life around Padstow.

Photographs:

All the photographs are from the author's collection with the exception of Page 49 which is from the collection of Fred Elton, St. Austell.

Barry Kinsmen
Padstow, 1997

PREFACE

I was very fortunate to grow up at a particular time in the history of our area, and my childhood was in many ways typical of those who grew up in the immediate post-war years. At that time Padstow was a predominantly Cornish community which had largely remained unchanged over the years.

The title of the book conveys my deep pride at being a Son of Padstow, for that community has been a source of great joy and support to me at many times in my life. I was so proud to be the Town Mayor in 1974-75 when under Local Government re-organisation, Padstow had a Mayor for the first time since the reign of Elizabeth I. It was during my time as Mayor that I was ordained and became the Non-Stipendiary Curate of the Parish Church.

There are so many people that I would like to thank for information and support in my preparation of this book. Members of my family, especially my cousin Jill, who typed the transcript of the book, often having to decipher my hand writing with difficulty. The people of Padstow who have inspired me to write about growing up there and my friends who have listened to me reading sections of the book to see if I have captured with sensitivity the mood of the town.

Richard Carew in his 'Survey of Cornwall' written in 1602 gave titles to various Cornish towns and he aptly sensed that there was a particular warmth in Padstow, which he crystallised in the phrase 'Good Fellowship of Padstow'. I dedicate this book to that Good Fellowship; long may it endure.

Town Mayor 1974-75

Reproduced from the 1946 Ordance Survey map

CHAPTER I

~ HAWKERS COVE IN FORMER TIMES ~

Were there ever Hawkers at Hawkers Cove? I wondered as I pondered and reflected on my early childhood in that small but very human community where I was born. Hawkers Cove is a small bay or inlet about half a mile inland from Stepper Point on the west bank of the River Camel. The name Camel derives from the Cornish words cam, crooked and hayle estuary. Crooked estuary is a fine description of this extensive expanse of water which has become choked with sand during the past five hundred years. It is the only estuary of any size on the rugged north coast of Cornwall.

The actual site of Hawkers Cove is relatively sheltered and it was near to the little bay, once stony but now sandy that six pilot cottages were built for the River and Sea Pilots of the Port of Padstow in the early years of the 1870's. These cottages with their long front gardens sloping down to the edge of the cliff were somewhat protected from the more extreme ravages of the wind which blows with great ferocity in this part of Cornwall. On average we have about thirty five gale's a year.

2

The Pilot Cottages are still at Hawkers Cove on the north side. They have become private holiday homes with only number six lived in all the year. At the head of the Cove and at the top of the beach is a modernised cottage which was once two cottages where lived in the hinds employed on the nearby farm of Lellizzick. Underneath this cottage was kept the original Padstow lifeboat 'The Mariners Friend'. Next to the cottage there was the Arab House so named because the Arab Lifeboat was once housed there. There was and still is a long slipway dipping down into the sea in front of the building. The house has been made into a boat house belonging to the cottage next door. The slipway was a favourite place for the children of Hawkers Cove to play.

The Pilot Cottages were later joined by another row of houses higher up from the sheltered cove. These were the coast guard houses built in the 1900 for those important men who constantly watched the cruel and capricious North Coast of Cornwall for ships in difficulty. There were seven houses in that row, six identical and a larger, grander house for the station officer. Next to this larger house was the office where the coast guard administration work was carried out. These houses were very much more exposed than the Pilot Cottages, and it was in number four that I was born.

As a baby in garden of 4 Pilot Cottages

I have often tried to imagine what the area around the Cove as we called Hawkers Cove, was like in times of pre-history. I had grown up with the knowledge the my paternal grandfather William Charles Kinsman (Charlie) had found some kind of burial urn in one of the fields near to the back of the farm house at Lelizzick where he had worked as a farm labourer. The urn was probably found in Middle Skin Field which was clearly shown on the Tithe Map of the parish. It was I believe a similar type of urn to those found at Harlyn Bay where a large Beaker Folk Cemetery was discovered in 1900.

My grandfather tried to unearth the urn but in his haste it broke into several pieces. He had an idea that these pieces might have formed part of a treasure hoard, so he took them home. They were kept in his house in Hawkers Cove until he enlisted in the army at the commencement of the First World War. My grandmother, who was very concerned at keeping the house tidy, used his absence as an excuse to throw away those dirty bits of stone as she called them.

There must have been some kind of prehistoric settlement on Lellizzick Farm. It could have been near to the Coastguard Station or even covering a much larger area. A large rampart and ditch stretches from Hawkers Cove to Butter Hole. It is most visible there where less ploughing has taken place. George Carlyle whose family farmed Lellizzick until recently found a stone lined grave in one of the fields adjacent to Butter Hole. A number of artifacts including an amulet and spindle whorls have been recovered from different parts of the 272 acres of Lellizzick Farm.

There were at least three of four barrows on the area around Stepper Point. It is most likely that people lived here since Mesolithic Times (8000BC) and so, near to Hawkers Cove there have been people from the time of pre history. Then the land mass was higher and the beautiful estuary of the Camel had not been formed. There is evidence of a submerged forest at Daymer Bay which may have covered the whole of the estuary mouth and Doom Bar in the period before the formation of the drowned Ria type estuary.

The barrows on Lellizzick date from the era of chamber tombs. They are less spectacular than Crugmeer (the Great Barrow) or Craigtoll (Barrow on the Brow). These massive tombs were covered with a huge mound of earth and were prepared and used for the chieftains of the local tribes.

It was exciting and a little frightening to know that for almost ten thousand years there had been people living near to my birthplace at Hawkers Cove.

It was in one of the coastguard houses that I was born on the 17th August, 1940. I was a small premature baby born some six weeks before time. I had no finger or toenails or so I am told. I weighed just over 4lbs and was considered to be lucky to be born alive. My mother had had a difficult pregnancy as she had been operated on for large fibroids while carrying me. I arrived in the world early and was a very lively and demanding baby. My mother had many sleepless nights while I was a baby and I was two years of age before I slept through the night. My mother was so surprised when this happened that she wondered if I had died during the first peaceful night she had experienced since my birth.

My birth certificate records the birth of Barry William the son of William Arnold Joseph and Winifred May Kinsmen.

Arnold was a chief stoker in the Royal Navy which he had just joined on leaving Padstow school and Winifred was a housewife. The small modernised cottage was originally built by the Padstow Harbour Association. It was they who encouraged the building of the first road to Hawkers Cove. The access in the early days of the Lifeboat Station was either by sea or footpath from Padstow. The most direct footpath was via Tregirls farm but the scenic route was the coastal path from Padstow passing by St.George's well and Battery Point. The children of Hawkers Cove walked to school each day via Tregirls Farm. The route involved a five mile round trip each day in all kinds of weather. When the weather was wet the children arrived at Padstow School (then Padstow Board School and later Padstow Council School) soaked to the skin. The wet clothes were dried on the guard around the tortoise stoves. This was not the ideal way to begin the school day. The road to Hawkers Cove was a private road until recent years. The last mile known as Tregudda Lane was full of deep pot holes and was often awash with surface water. It was a driver's nightmare driving along this stretch of road where at one time there were at least a dozen gates to open. When the Padstow Town Council took over the lease of the Coastguard Houses the road became a public road and so was adopted and maintained being tarmaced with proper drainage channels at each side of the road.

The road passes by the ancient farmhouse of Lellizzick Farm. This farm formed part of the Barton of Lellizzick which included the greenstone headland of Stepper Point. The Barton was used for hunting in mediaeval times when under the ownership of the Priory of Bodmin. It was said to be a favourite haunt of the Prior. At the time of the Reformation the land passed to the Prideaux family who still own it. In 1634 the farm bore the name of Lanlesick (Lan church or cell Lesick or Losek, wood or bushy) - the cell in the wood.

It is from the gate beyond the farmhouse at Lellizzick that the whole panoramic view of the estuary is revealed. The settlement of the Cove appears in the foreground, while the Doom Bar and the whole of the estuary lies spread out before you. Across the estuary can be seen Daymer Bay, Brae Hill and the once buried Chapel of ease of St. Enodoc with it's tiny spire peeping up from the sand dunes. The church was once known to local people as 'Sinking Neddy', a term of affection. The beauty and grandeur of the scenery at Cove inculcated in me a deep love of the estuary which has played such a large part in my life.

The road drops sharply from the farm and many motorists have been taken by surprise by the descent which ends with a very sharp hairpin bend. The descent allows you to see why there was a settlement here from earliest time. The valley which runs through St. Samson field afforded shelter in an area where it is a rare commodity.

The road reaches the bottom of the hill where there is a small turning area, it then continues through a gate which was always kept shut marking the boundary of the Coastguard Station. It was only open for vehicles which were bound there. As children were always instructed to keep the gate firmly shut. Beyond the gate was the Church of Good Shepherd on the left while on the right was a large store, used partly by the Coastguards, which contained the life saving equipment and the Breeches Buoy. The other part was used by them to store fishing tackle and crab pots. The crabpots were made by them while sitting on the steps leading to the store. I can still picture John Baker and Jack England skillfully making or mending the pots while the warm sun beat down on their browned and weather beaten faces. The crabpots formed part of the Harvest Thanksgiving decorations in the church.

At the side of the turning space was a red postbox which was emptied daily by the postman from Padstow, but when I was a small child the letters were collected by the postlady who walked, in all weathers, all the way from Padstow delivering the mail, which included small parcels.

Three steps led down from the turning space onto the path from the small cottage which wended its way to the Pilot Houses. At the front of the steps was a chute which carried the stream and water draining from Chapel Field. Chapel Field was a very undulating field, basically two steep slopes on either side of the valley through which flowed a stream from a spring at its head. The stream was piped under the road by the chute.

This field and the neighbouring field of St. Samson played an important part in the life of the parish. The Tithe Apportionment Map and accompanying schedule, made in December 1840, recorded Chapel Field as being an arable field of just over 13 acres. The name implies, and history testifies, to the existence of an ancient chapel in or near the field.

Among the papers of Charles Henderson, the great Cornish historian whose life was tragically cut short by his untimely death at the age of 34, was a crumpled old map of 1694 which formed part of the Prideaux-Brune estate papers. It was John Prideaux Esq who commissioned George Withiell to produce it. It shows the chapel as a small rectangular building with a cross on the east gable situated by the stream.

The six inch ordnance survey map issued in 1905, but surveyed much earlier in 1879-80, locates the chapel someway up the valley on the south side of the stream which flows from the nearby spring.

It was probably the mediaeval chapel of St. Samson although the field to the north towards Stepper Point now behind the Coastguard Station bears his name. It could be that these two fields were originally a single one. There are no remains of the chapel today, but it is probable that some vestige remained until about a hundred years ago. The late Bob England, who was a pilot and lived at the Cove at the turn of the century, remembered an old cob wall standing on a small flat area near the source to the spring. The wall formed part of a building approximately thirty feet long by twenty feet wide which was once used as a pig's house by the late Mr. William Magor. This can only be an assumption although Mr. George Carlyle found, some forty years ago, pieces of worked catacleuse stone which could have been used for the under sills of the windows of the chapel.

St. Samson was one of the two most important chapels in the Parish of Padstow. It probably was in use until the Reformation and the dissolution of the monasteries when the offerings made here were transferred from the Priory of Bodmin to the new secular Lords. After the Reformation the Chapel ceased to be used and gradually fell into a ruinous state.

The cell of St. Samson was somewhere in the vicinity of Hawkers Cove. Samson, like Bishop Wethenoc, was in residence prior to the coming of St. Petroc in the early years of the sixth century. Petroc sailed up the estuary after crossing from Ireland to begin his extensive campaign of evangelisation to the people of this area. Samson and Wethinoc vacated their cells and left the field clear for the work of St. Petroc.

Samson moved to South Hill near Callington where, incidentally, the Kinsman family lived at one time, and finally to Dol in Brittany, where he is still commemorated.

We return to the path to the house at Hawkers Cove. The chute carrying the water from Chapel Field emerged into a large stone trough. The water here was crystal clear although there were ferns and various pond weeds growing in the trough. The water was originally used as the source of drinking water for the cottages opposite. We washed our wellington boots there after the long walk from Padstow. Near to the trough a tap had been placed which was used by the cottagers, flower arrangers in the church and the fishermen who worked in the stores nearby.

It was the formation of the Padstow Harbour Association during the early years of the nineteenth century which gave impetus to the development of the cove.

One of the greatest needs was that of the lifeboat. The estuary of the River Camel was the only sizeable

Hawkers Cove - left Coastguard Station, right Pilot Cottages, Mission Church in front

estuary or inlet on the perilous North Coast of Cornwall. Lloyds' agent at Padstow who kept a record of vessels wrecked on the coast between Perranporth and Bude, listed, between 1800 and 1826, the demise of over a hundred vessels either wrecked or stranded here. The old rhyme which most of us learnt as children about the cruel nature of our coast was never more true.

"From Padstow Point to Lundy Light
Is a sailor's grave by day or night".

It was largely due to the efforts of a certain Commander Williams, who was probably the chief officer of the Coastguards in the 1820's, that Padstow acquired its first lifeboat.

This worthy and respected gentleman worked indefatigably towards this end and and raised £30 towards the cost of a lifeboat for the town. When the Royal National Lifeboat Institution became aware of his sterling effort they sanctioned the giving of £10 as a grant. This was in January 1827 and made possible the building of the first lifeboat, the Mariners Friend, which was built by John Tredwen in his shipyard at Padstow. The final cost being £50. She was a four oared 'gig' type boat. Originally she was kept in Padstow Quay but in 1829 was moved to Hawkers Cove, being housed in a stone building near to high water. This was probably the cottage with a large cellar or room underneath. It is situated at the head of the actual cove and has, subsequently, been modernised. The room had a dimension of thirty feet by twenty feet so the boat, which was 23ft in length, could comfortably fit into it. The lifeboat was kept on a carriage which enabled her to be launched at all tides, for there were times when it was necessary to use it, particularly when the tide was low. The stone cottage (or cottages,as they were originally two) was shown on the Tithe Map of 1840 as the only building besides that of the chapel near to Hawkers Cove. The accompanying schedule records the house and its small garden. When my grandparents came to Hawkers Cove in 1910 the cottages were still two. My grandfather worked on Lelissick Farm and the cottage must have been very small for his growing family. They already had four children, Dorothy Lillian born in 1903, Lottie Kathleen Elsie in1905, Beatrice Laura in 1908 and my father, William Arnold Joseph, in1909. They were not in that small cottage for long because they moved into number four Pilot Cottages before the birth of the twins, Edward Claude and Helena Louie Wood, in 1912. Their youngest child, Ida Louvain, being born in1915. You will meet them later in the book

Hawkers Cove with the Arab House and slipway. Farm labourer's cottage with original lifeboat house underneath

but I must explain that Kathleen, Arnold and Louvain answered to the second christian names, as is often the case in many parts of Cornwall and Lena was never called Helena.

The cottage was very sheltered and when my Aunty Beat and Uncle Fred lived there in the late 1940s and early 1950s there was still no water indoors and they fetched all the water from the nearby tap. The cellar has long ceased being used as the lifeboat house but you could hear the sea as it ran into the large cellar where once the Mariners Friend was housed. The house was consequently very damp.

Let us continue to follow the path to the Pilot Cottages. It then made its way across the slope which led down to the beach at Hawkers Cove passing in front of the large house where the Pilot Boats were once kept..

The descent to the stony beach was steep and on the left under the cliff where Valerian (Padstow Pride) and ivy grew in profusion where the punts, often pulled up safely above the high water level for the winter. Aunty Kath's yellow punt was among them. In the early spring the boats were prepared for their re-entry into the sea and on these warm spring days which we seemed to have when I was a child the smell of paint and tar filled the air.

On the right was the Arab house, so named because it once housed the Arab lifeboat. It was largely demolished some years ago but has been rebuilt as a boat store. On the edge of the water were round pebbles of all sizes and thicknesses. The thinner ones were ideal for skimming along the surface of the water. There was always competition between the children of the Cove to see how many times you could skim them before thy sank beneath the waves. Most of our pleasures as children were simple ones which children had participated in for generations. In the immediate post war years we still lived in times of great austerity.

The Arab house, as we called it, was not originally built for the Arab but for Albert Edward II. This house was constructed in 1864 and replaced the original lifeboat house under the neighbouring cottage. At the front of the house was a long slipway down which the boat was launched. The cost of building the house and the slipway was £273 and it served as the lifeboat's residence until 1931 when a new building was erected on the south side of the cove at the beginning of the path to Tregirls cove.

The Arab house had large black doors into which were set a smaller door. This door opened into pitch darkness. We often peeped into this house with a certain degree of apprehension wondering what might be lurking in the sheer darkness there. One thing was certain, there was a distinctive smell of oil and grease inside. It was at that time used for the chainboat which was used to maintain the machinery which assisted the launching of the lifeboat.

Before we continue our walk to the Pilot Houses we must see how the formation of the Padstow Harbour Association in 1829 gave impetus to the development of Hawkers Cove. The association was a logical step in the evolution of the port. It began its life at a public meeting held on the 11th November 1829 when its title was proudly described as 'The Association for the Preservation of Life and Property from Shipwreck'. Its patron was the Reverend Charles Prideaux-Brune.

The importance of the Port of Padstow was shown by the wide support given from the diverse group of subscribers. The internationally famous Lloyd's Agency gave £100 and various Cornish gentry, merchants and shipowners were found to be on the subscribers list. Donations were not confined to the Duchy. The Merchant Venturers Society of Bristol, along with other persons involved in the prosperous coastal trade with Bristol and South Wales, added their names to the list. The organisation was then entirely supported by voluntary contributions.

One of the first actions of the new organisation was to build a large tower near to the coast on Stepper Point. This was the Daymark which served as a warning by day to ships sailing near the rugged but dangerous coast of Stepper Point. The Daymark, which is now in a less than satisfactory condition, is forty feet in height and is about a quarter of a mile west of Stepper Point standing on the edge of the cliff which, incidentally, is at that point some 254 feet above sea level. In clear weather the Beacon or Daymark can be seen by vessels up to twenty-four miles from the coast. The Padstow Harbour Association balance sheet for 1832 states "paid in part for a Daymark built on the Beacon as per contract £29".

When we as children walked up hill, as the area near to the Daymark was known, there were always a large number of rabbits scampering around leaving behind them 'currents' which were, of course, their small droppings. The rabbits played around the large bushes of yellow gorse which grew in profusion on the rough soil there. Next to the Daymark was a small building erected and used as part of the coastal defences during the last war. This had a small fence around and was clearly defined 'private property'. We could play in the Daymark. It was exciting to look up at the sky through the top which was like a gigantic telescope. In the side were set windows or, more technically, open spaces. The wind howled through these and the interior of the Daymark had a cold eerie feeling about it.

In 1830 a Branch of Pilots for the Port of Padstow was established. The Elder Brethren of Trinity House had been successfully lobbied by Captain Julian R.N. on behalf of the Padstow Harbour Association. The first Sub Commissioners of Pilotage were appointed. It was vital to have Pilots to escort vessels in and out of the Port of Padstow, for as Pigots Directory of 1830 records, there were seventy vessels registered there.

The Pilots lived in private houses in Padstow until the row of Pilot Houses were built at Hawkers Cove as part of the improvements made to the port.

The Harbour Association positioned three large capstans on the inner side of Stepper Point and moored two buoys in the channel which was at that time located on the west side of the estuary running close in under Stepper Point and past Hawkers Cove, Tregirls Beach and round Battery Point. Indeed, in my childhood there was always water off the Cove and it was only at low tide when spring tides were at their lowest that we could wade across to the Bar. The whole development of Hawkers Cove depended on ready access at all times. The departure of the lifeboat from Cove was the result of the gradual disappearance of the main channel from the west side of the estuary.

Hawkers Cove was connected by road with Crugmeer and Padstow allowing vehicular access to the lifeboat station. Before this time, and indeed even well into the early years of the century, lifeboatmen had to run from Padstow via Tregirls farm when the rockets were set off, warning of a ship in distress. The rockets were fired on the green of the Coastguard Station at Cove and also at Padstow at one time.

There was no doubt that Padstow Harbour Association was a great asset to the port. Henry Peter Rawlings who presided at the first annual general meeting was able to tell the meeting that six vessels had been saved from total wreck. They were from a variety of ports. The Sloop Thomas from Falmouth, the Sloop Mary and Ann Elizabeth from London, the Schooner Stephen Knight of Plymouth, the Brig Spectacular of Exeter, the Brig Violet of Arundle and there was a local boat the Schooner Pamona of Padstow.

The names of vessels saved and rescued by the lifeboat were household words in Pilot Cottages. There was a tremendous and justifiable pride among the lifeboatmen, many of whom were also river and sea pilots. The womenfolk played their part too having hot refreshments ready for the menfolk when they returned. On a number of occasions the women also helped with the launching of the Arab from its house. The women knew what it was to endure hardship and had to work in a way that today would hardly be believed. Hardship bound the little community of Cove together.

In 1830 a substantial six oared gig, well calculated for heavy seas, was obtained at a cost of £20-11s and was kept near to Stepper Point, possibly at Cove. It was used for taking out hawsers and other hobbling work.

In 1844, the year that my great grandfather, Joseph Hooper, was born across the estuary at Trenain Farm (then known as Downathan), the Padstow Harbour Act was passed by parliament. The cost of acquiring this important Act was £1703-17s-7d. The wording of the Act implied its purpose 'for regulating, maintaining and improving the Port of Padstow...... and the navigable parts of the River Camel or Alan in the same county'. Charles Prideaux-Brune conveyed to the Padstow Harbour Commissioners, who were elected as a result of the Act, the quay and the rights to the tolls of the harbour. One of the major problems facing ships entering the harbour was the baffling winds under Stepper Point and in 1868-69 application was made for the provisional order to alter the point by cutting down a portion of the bluff at Stepper Point. This recommendation came out of the Royal Commission on setting up a Harbour of Refuge on the North Coast of Cornwall. The need for this was undoubted but it never happened. The Commission did, however, recommend that the the Harbour should be improved and that the Commissioners should lease part of the field known as Clowter which is located on the extremity of Stepper Point. This action was to allow them to deal with the problem of the baffling winds by reducing the bluff which formed part of the field.

The need for cottages for the Pilots to live in at Hawkers Cove was recognised and the Association sought to lease about three acres from the Prideaux-Brune Estate for a term of seventy-two years from 25th September 1869 to build six or more cottages for Pilots or Boatmen. These dwellings were to be let by the Association. So the Pilot Cottages were built at the edge of Chapel Field on the north side of Hawkers Cove. Later the coastguard Houses were also built within the boundaries of the field. I have already explained why the field bore that name. As a child I found the names of fields around Hawkers Cove a real interest. As soon as I knew that all the fields on Lellizzick Farm had particular names my mother was pestered with an unending series of questions about each field and its name.

It was in Chapel Field where we often played as children that the Pilot Cottages, the small cottage and original lifeboat house and, later, the Coastguard Station were built. One of my favourite pastimes as a small child was to jump the narrow stream which ran down the valley of the field. We as children would frequently do this but on one occasion while playing with a parachute made by one of my childhood friends, Brian England, I landed smack in the middle of the stream. I then had the task of trying to clean myself up before returning home to explain to my mother how I became covered with mud from head to tail. The hardest part of the explanation was to account for the mud and weed in the inside of my wellingtons.

If the weather was wet and windy, as it often was and is in this part of Cornwall, I would be dressed up in wellington boots, macintosh and sou-wester as I loved playing in the rain and mist.

It was across this narrow valley that the Coastguards had their life saving practice with Breeches Buoy. The Buoy was shot across the valley and it was handed back with a coastguard in it. I cannot ever remember seeing it being used for sea rescue at Cove. The decision made recently to scrap its use would have bought great sadness to that generation of coastguards.

Although Padstow never became a harbour of refuge, the Pilot Cottages were built and completed by the early 1870s. The Pilots must have been very busy, for in 1871 the Pilots piloted from Stepper Point to the harbour in Padstow, three hundred and twenty-four coasters, four British overseas vessels and twelve foreigners, making a total of three hundred and thirty-eight boats. These paid £156 in harbour dues.

The pilots also escorted one hundred and fourteen vessels out of the port. The pilots were registered by Trinity House and had to pay one guinea a year for the use of the river. The payment was made on January 31st which the Pilots at Cove called 'Guinea Day'.

The problem of the Doom Bar was one of the most difficult facing the Padstow Harbour Association. In 1881 Mr. Silas Nicholls, a local engineer, conceived a scheme for clearing the Doom Bar of sand by making a tunnel from Butter Hole through Lellizzick Farm to Hawkers Cove. This would have been a very expensive scheme and would have radically altered Hawkers Cove. The cost being prohibitive, it was never proceeded with. There was a small gate beyond the fisherman's store which led into the driveway to the Coastguard Houses built in 1900. Before that time the Coastguards had lived in Padstow but it seemed sensible to have them near to the estuary mouth, so they joined the Pilots at Cove. While in Padstow they lived in various places, one of which was High St. At the end of the nineteenth century the Chief of coastguard lived in the house called Clent, which is opposite the Parish Church in Church St. Henry Farris, who was the chief coastguard, lived here in 1892 as did his successor, John Bolt, in 1897. John's son was one of the earliest possessers of a boy's penny farthing bicycle. The late Walton Hicks remembered that when the tyres wore out the coastguards made rope tyres for the vehicle.

The first Chief Officer to live at the Coastguard Station was George Livingstone. The coastguards at Cove had the responsibility of overseeing the section of coast between Trevose Head and Port Isaac which were the neighbouring stations.

The gardens of the Coastguard Houses were meticulously maintained in my childhood. On the lawn area south of the houses was the tall flagpole from which the storm cone was hoisted whenever gale warnings were issued. One of the pranks which we as children took part in was being hoisted upwards in the black cone. The prank usually ended with a stentorian shout from the coastguard on duty or the Coastguard Officer, Mr. Millard, whose dining room faced the green. The shout was a stern warning of danger of this exercise. This was the signal to be let down the cone, jump out, and run as quickly as possible for the nearby stile which led to safety. If you reached the stile you could either run down the side of Iron Cove to the Watch House or double back under the tamarisk hedge which separated the gardens of the Pilot Houses from the Coastguard Station. The tamarisk hedge was used by the children to build a tree house or camp in.

Once more we returned to the path, for beyond the Cove the path divided. One section ran along the top of the cliff at the foot of the long front gardens of the Pilot Houses. This was once the main entrance to them, but it is now completely overgrown with brambles and other shrubs and unusable. The other path made its way to the back of the houses. On either side of the path were veronica and escallonia hedges. The leaves of the latter were sticky and had an attractive scent. The path on reaching the first of the houses, which was lived in by Joe and Lena Wills when I was a child, widened to become 'the cement'. The cement was a flat area about three feet in width with a gully by the side. Three taps were strategically placed for the inhabitants of the six houses to collect water which was used for cleaning purposes. The gully or drain carried all the waste water which was thrown out from the houses to the edge of the cliff where it cascaded over the cliff in a miniature waterfall. My grandmother's section was scrubbed every day and Jeyes fluid was poured into it to keep it clean. The cement was cold and very windy, especially when the bitter north or east wind blew. There was a marked contrast between it and the warm south facing front of the house. it was basically cruel and inhospitable, especially in winter. If you had been a visitor in times past you would have approached the pilot houses by sea or, if you were walking, you would have taken the narrow path which was in front of the gardens along the cliff edge. Each of the Pilot Houses had a large garden in front and behind and a further garden behind the pighouses and closet facing eastwards across the estuary. The narrow path in front of the houses is now overgrown and invisible but it once was the front entrance to the stone built cottages. The front gardens of the cottages with their southerly aspect were a sun trap and flowers grew in profusion in them. The Kinsman's garden was beautiful, reflecting hours of loving care on the part of the family. The Kinsmans had green fingers and a great love of plants, especially flowers and shrubs. By the time I was a child a large veronica hedge separated the garden from those of the neighbouring houses. The front garden had been terraced by Aunty Kath.

The garden was full of interest so let us start from the hedge adjacent to the edge of the cliff. A white

Family picnic

gate into the garden proclaimed the house to be Mer Vue. The French connection seemed strange in so Cornish a place. Aunty Kath and Gran had been very friendly with the Breton Crabbers who frequently fished off the North Coast of Cornwall. Indeed during the German occupation of France a number of them made their home in Padstow. Jules Mevel and his family from Camaret near Brest often visited the house at Cove. During the war the family stored the Mevel's best linen for them. The title 'Mer Vue' was a little pretentious, a sign of the families pride. It was good to have a name for the house, a foreign name at that. I visited Jules when holidaying in Brittany in 1973. He was by then a widower living in a tiny villa above the small fishing town of Camaret. He was delighted to see me and talked about the happy times spent with the family at Cove. I well remember as a child seeing a number of clogs left outside the front door of the house. I also remember the rather rough 'Vin Ordinaire' that the Frenchmen drank, being consumed in the front room of the house.

The warm southerly aspect of the garden made it a favourite place to sunbathe. You were surrounded by a great variety of flowers, gladiolus of various colours, phlox, stocks, godetias, carnations and pinks were among the favoured plants. Immediately under the front room window was a large grape vine although I suspect it was probably barren and never produced any fruit. A large rain water tank was also found by the window nearest to the west hedge of the garden, this was the source of the water used in the house for many years.

The front door of the house was reached by climbing three stone and slate steps, a favourite place for sitting in the warm sunshine. The memory of the intense heat of the steps on a hot summer day on my bare legs as a child remains with me to this day. I often dream that I am sitting on those steps with the marvellous and extensive view in my mind's eye. In the immediate foreground was the last of the lifeboat houses built in 1931 to contain the number two Padstow lifeboat which was used for ships or people in distress within the estuary. Next to the lifeboat was a small wooden and rather rickety landing stage used by the smaller boats which frequented the Cove. It was from this stage that an elderly man (named Duncan) from Trevone committed suicide. My grandmother saw this from the front room window and my aunt was pretty certain that the shock of this caused the first of many strokes which my grandmother suffered.

The children of Hawkers Cove used the wooden stage as a diving base. They were expert swimmers and divers, which I was not. I could swim but I was never a strong swimmer. While my friends swam like fishes and dived like birds I was content to sit on the hard rocks in the sunshine with my nose in a book. I was a bookworm and never a practical child. I can still barely drive a nail straight into a piece of wood. My world was the world of ideas, and of people. I envied people who had the practical skills which make life so much easier. The footpath to Padstow which skirted the Cove was directly opposite the Pilot Cottages and so you could see from the vantage point everyone who came to Hawkers Cove as you sat on the warm step. The path from the number two lifeboathouse which passed between two hedges where blackberry and sloes grew in abundance was known as Dick's piece. This probably referred to the small garden above the path belonging to the farm labourer's cottage. Who Dick was had long been forgotten and I have never been able to find out. This was one of the unsolved mysteries of my childhood.

At the end of Dick's piece was a small wooden gate from where the path entered Hay Field. The path

Hawkers Cove from Tregirls Beach.

continued along the cliff edge for the length of the field passing a pear tree on its seaward side. There were small rails placed at any points where the path was dangerously near the edge of the small cliff. At the top of the cliff were large clumps of sea pinks and soft springy grass making this a favourite place for picnics. You could picnic there without getting bits of sand in the sandwiches. I was a fussy and fastidious child, and grains of sand were never an acceptable part of my diet.

Tregirls Beach or Harbour Cove (which was the name shown on all the maps) was a favourite place for the Padstownians to go beaching. At that time the tide covered the large, flat, sandy beach cleaning it at every tide. It was around the cliff and across this beach that the children of Hawkers Cove walked daily to and from Padstow school. Often they would have to run between the waves avoiding getting wet feet and spending a miserable day in damp clothes at school. It was a long and tiring walk for the youngest of the children often only barely five years of age. In mid-winter the children left home when the dawn had barely broken and returned as the mantle of dusk fell. No wonder so many of the family suffered from arthritis from mid-life onwards.

At the far side of the beach were Tregirls fields. The large fields with a steep path climbing ever upwards to Tregirls Farm. It was an exhausting climb up these two fields but you were rewarded with a truly breathtaking view from the gate and stile leading into Tregirls Lane. The whole of the estuary mouth lay spread out before you with two large headlands of Stepper and Pentire guarding the wide estuary mouth. The tired and weary walker returning home from Cove knew that when Tregirls Farm was reached, it was downhill all the way. The lights of the two rows of cottages beckoned the walkers ever onwards. We usually walked this way to Padstow for after my father was killed we had no car. My mother struggled with the shopping bought in Padstow never complaining of the hardship which life had dealt her. As I grew older I realised how selfless she had been through the years of my childhood and indeed to the end of her life. She was so young when widowed, only thirty-three, and she bore the forty-one years of her widowhood bravely.

It is difficult to remember which of my many experiences and memories of life was the earliest I recollect. I find it hard to differentiate between what I actually remember and what I have been told by the members of my family. It was certain that I was not an easy child to bring up. I have already mentioned that I was two years of age before I slept the night through. My mind was over active and that was the verdict of Dr. Sheldon, our family doctor. He was extremely good with children and my mother had great confidence in him. It was he who was present at my birth. It was he who came to Cove when I swallowed a large amount of camphorated oil and on another occasion when a large pea was stuck up my nostril. It was a long walk for him.

The wonder of my childhood was the patience of my mother, for I had an insatiable desire for knowledge. She was bombarded by an endless stream of questions - Why? What? How? It was good that she understood that this was how children learn. She would have made an excellent teacher. Indeed this is what she wanted to be at one time. Her father had other ideas as he feared his only daughter might turn out to be a dominant and somewhat crabby person like his Aunt-by-marriage, Amy, who taught in Forest Gate in London.

One of my earliest memories was being given a broken alarm clock which provided me an excellent way of learning to tell the time. I was then about three and a half years of age and my new found skill caused a great surprise to a group of coastguard wives sitting on the slate slab covering the old well which was situated near to the front of the Coastguard Station. They must have been discussing the time and I said rather precociously, 'it is half past three', which of course it was. One of the ladies, I forget which one, hastily rushed into her house to look at the clock. As she came out again she was heard to exclaim, 'You'd never believe it but the little bugger's right'.

Another of my favourite play things was a set of rubber letters which I played with for hours on a rug in the living room of number four Coastguard Station. These letters were made into words by me. 'Does this spell house ?' 'Does this say book?' My poor mother, engaged in housework or cooking, patiently answered 'yes' and occasionally 'no'. I know realise that I rarely saw her sitting down as there was so much to do and not much money to do it with. Her savings were rapidly used up in the years following my father's death. She was not able to buy new clothes for herself although I had them. It must have been when she started working that she could afford one or two new things for herself. It was ironic that my mother, who had a good commercial training and was an outstanding typist and skilled at shorthand, lived in an area where these skills were not in great demand.

I have only scant memories of my father, which I will be mentioning. It was difficult until I grew older to find out about him. My mother talked little about it for she found it almost impossible to do so as her bereavement went deep. My grandmother Kinsman and Aunty Kath would have talked more but they knew my mother's feelings so well. I know they thought she should talk more about him and in some way give vent to her inner grief. She just couldn't talk freely about her sadness and loss. She was a very private person who didn't wear her emotions on her sleeve.

My fascination for clocks had amusing consequences on one of my visits to London. I think it was the last Christmas before I started school. My mother and I had gone to London to stay with my grandparents. My grandfather's office had been evacuated to Harefield in Middlesex. The lady in whose house he stayed was a Welsh lady named Mrs. James. She had an alarm clock which worked when I was allowed to take it to the local church or chapel where a performance of the Messiah was taking place. Unfortunately during one of the solo items I set the alarm off. Great was the embarrassment of my family.

CHAPTER II

~ NUMBER FOUR PILOT HOUSES ~
- The Kitchen -

The back doors of all the houses opened off the cement. You passed three of them before you arrived at Number Four. The family all remembered the excitement of going home to Cove and the house where my grandparents raised their seven children and even when I had long since left Cove, there was a great sense of excitement as I approached the back door of Number Four. The back door was painted green with a small brass oval door knob which shone from frequent applications of Brasso. The knob was loose and ill fitting but still functional. Outside the door was a doormat and scraper where you could clean the mud off shoes, sea boots and wellingtons before entering the house. This was a very necessary operation in the county where most paths were muddy in all but the driest of weathers. The door was seldom locked when the Kinsman family were young or even when I was a child for it was rare to bolt doors even at night. Most houses were open to friends and neighbours at all times.

No doubt the door was locked and the curtains drawn on Saturday evenings when my father, his brother and sisters bathed in front of the black leaded stove in the kitchen. The tin baths were taken down from the walls of the pantry where they hung on hooks, filled with hot water from the copper and placed in front of the stove. This was the usual routine in most households, for it was important to be clean for Sundays when best clothes were usually worn.

The cold cement was soon forgotten when you opened the door and entered the small and extremely draughty kitchen. On opening the door you shouted, 'Coo-ee', and called out your name so that Gran or Aunty Kath knew who had come. It was highly unlikely however, that your approach had not been noticed, for from the moment you came in sight of the Cove, Aunty Kath would fix the old binoculars on you so that she could chart the progress of the approaching walkers. She loved the binoculars which we thought she used to watch courting couples on the cliffs. During the 2nd World War she would train them on the guns which were placed at Battery Point as part of the coastal defences.

The back door was ill fitting and the draught blew strongly under the bottom of it. Behind the door hung numerous old coats which served a two fold purpose, that of helping to keep out draughts and also being available for outdoor use. Gran would wrap an old coat around her shoulders when she sallied forth for the bucket lavatories on the edge of the cliff. Aunty Kath would wear one of them when she gardened as she did for hours each day in one of the three gardens belonging to the houses.

In the left hand corner behind the door were walking sticks and an assortment of brooms and brushes. The motto of this house would have endeared itself to the great apostle of Methodism, John Wesley, who declared, 'cleanliness was next to Godliness'. The Kinsmans were house proud and no greater disgrace could befall them than to be visited when the house was not clean and polished and the beds made. It was said that my grandmother would even polish the coal if given a chance.

A large old wardrobe full of good clothes, coats and hats and other garments filled the rest of the wall which separated the kitchen from the even smaller pantry. The wardrobe contained a large drawer where the best tablecloths were kept. On top of the wardrobes were kept the suitcases which were meticulously packed whenever Gran or Aunty Kath left Cove to visit other members of the family. Next to the wardrobe was the door to the pantry and on the south wall of the kitchen was the door to the front room. You had to be extremely careful not to open the pantry door before closing the front room door or you would scratch the paint on one of them. This was another heinous crime.

Two green covered chairs with covered backs and an ancient easy chair stood against the front room wall. Above the chairs was hung the portrait of Great Uncle Claude, the youngest of the three Kinsman brothers. He was a good natured and attractive man whose life was cut short as a result of gassing incurred during the First World War. Mustard gas ate away the lungs of so many men in their prime. He lived for a few years after this tragedy. Gradually, however, his breathing became more and more laboured and he contracted TB, and, although after the First World War he worked for a short period on Lellizzick Farm and lodged with the family, eventually he could not work. It was typical of my grandparents to take Claude in, for the house at Cove was a place of refuge for relations who needed homes. Claude never married probably due to his illness.

The other portrait in the kitchen was that of Great Uncle Jabez, my grandfathers other brother. Jabez and Claude and my grandfather were very alike as were all the men in the Kinsman family. As a child I would gaze at the portraits after being told that I was a 'proper Kinsman', and to see if there was a definite likeness between us which there undoubtedly was. Poor Jabez was lost at the battle of Jutland soon after his marriage. I knew very little of him except that he was married and had no children.

The black-leaded kitchen range made by Oatey and Martyn of Wadebridge took up most of the wall at right angles to the back door. It was actually across the corner from the front room wall to the wall

Pilot Cottages - No. 4 my grandmother Kinsman's home (figure in doorway)

behind the electric cooker. It was not used for cooking by the time I was a child. It had however, served as the only means of providing hot meals when my grandmother bought up her family. All the delicious pasties, cakes and roast dinners were then cooked in the range. It was regularly cleaned and black-leaded though it was no longer in use.

There was a mantlepiece above the range with a number of items including two white spaniel dogs which guarded each end of it. Two brass candlesticks, a tea tin and a mirror jostled for position along the mantle. The other prized possession was a miniature coal scuttle made out of war-time shell cases by my grandfather who was in the Royal Garrison Artillery.

The shells were brought back from France or Belgium after the First World War. I knew little of his war record except that he must have been at Louvain when his youngest daughter was born. Several people in Padstow called their children after battle sites of the war to end all wars which took such a toll of human life. One of the disadvantages of having one of these names was that it was easy to work out the age of the owner.

On top of the black stove stood Aunty kath's pressure cooker. This was used to heat the chicken food. She loved to buy new items for the house. She spent much time scanning the pages of J.D. Williams or Oxendales catalogues to see the latest fashions or pieces of household ware. The advent of commercial television brought a new world of goods into her home.

She rarely was able to visit shops especially the larger ones found in the major towns. The routine groceries were ordered weekly from Reeves Grocery Shop in Padstow. Each week one of the employees would cycle to Cove to fetch the orders. The order book would be prepared before the person arrived and carefully checked when he or she came. Later in the week the goods would be delivered and cere-moniously ticked off item by item to see that the whole order was there.

My aunt and grandmother loved people to call. They knew roughly what day and time each week the various callers came. A cup of tea and some home made delicacy, usually a yeast bun, a powder bun, or piece of carraway seed cake would be preferred to the caller. It would be a major disgrace not to have home made cakes ready for guests or callers. They did not offer 'boughten traad' to them, not even a shop biscuit. The caller would provide an opportunity to learn what was going on 'up town' as Padstow has always been referred to. While my grandmother was never a gossip, she liked to hear about what was happening 'up town' which she rarely visited. Her travels were mainly to see her children and their families or occasionally to visit the doctor or dentist.

It was essential on these occasions to put on your best clothes and clean underwear. The family all regarded it as vital to have good clean underclothes when you went on a journey or visited friends in case you were involved in an accident or had to be taken to hospital. The gravest sin would be to arrive at the pearly gates with dirty knickers or pants with a hole in. Respectability went deeper than appearances.

Next to the range was an electric cooker which was, by the end of the Second War, the method of cooking. Electricity came to Hawkers Cove in 1939 but it was only the kitchen and front room which were wired until many years later. The stove seemed to work overtime and each day a cooked meal was prepared even when my grandmother was elderly. One of the strangest smells of my childhood was that of crab legs boiling in an old fashioned saucepan on the cooker which was often mixed with another nasty odour produced by the boiling of potato skins and other items for the fowls, in an old iron cooking pot. Houses seemed to have stronger and more distinctive smells.

The pressure cooker was used for boiling potato skins and chickens food. My mother was rather frightened of it and she had good reason to be. One afternoon she was visiting my aunt soon after she bought it. The pressure cooker as usual hissed angrily on top of the black leaded stove. My mother enquired cautiously as to whether it was performing normally. She knew better than to be too direct with Aunty Kath who considered herself to be an expert on everything. Her reply was quick and to the point. 'There's nothing wrong with the pressure cooker'. My mother and aunt went into the front room where Gran was sitting in her usual armchair by the fireside. They began chatting about various scraps of family news. Suddenly there was a massive explosion, my mother almost jumped out of her skin and Aunty Kath screamed only as she could do. Her screams and laughter were well known at Cove. They rushed into the kitchen where the scene awaiting them was one of total mayhem. The contents of the pressure cooker, mostly potato peelings and other left overs from dinner, were plastered over the black beams and the curtains. The ticker tape welcome given to important dignitaries in New York had nothing on the festoons found in the kitchen that day. My mother as usual did not comment.

On the low window ledge was a huge maiden hair fern in a decorated china pot. The fern grew larger and larger through each year of my childhood. Most of the family grew a similar type of fern in their homes. You did not have to be a particularly astute observer of human nature to see how she had moulded her children in their views and attitudes. By the side of the fern stood an oil lamp which had been the means of lighting the room before the advent of electricity. Small night lights were used upstairs and a candle was carried upstairs when you went to bed.

In front and against the window ledge was the kitchen table, covered with a green cloth. This was where the family ate as children except on Sundays and at Christmas when the front room was used. By the time I was a child all meals were eaten in the front room.

The family sat at this table on a long black wooden bench which was relegated to the passage when the children left home. While they ate silence was the rule of the house. My grandmother's cane hung at the side of the black leaded stove on the mantlepiece and was used whenever a child dared to break this rule.

The table was used to roll out the pastry. I can picture Aunty Kath vigorously rolling out her pastry on a pastry board and also using the table to iron the clothes which were invariably washed on Monday. The clothes were aired on the airer in the passage which was operated by a pulley. If the weather was wet the clothes were dried in front of the fire in the front room. Flies loved the house and I dreaded the large blue bottles or 'blow flies' which buzzed around the room skillfully avoiding the brown sticky fly papers hung from the beams. I had heard date pastries described as fly dirt and I imagined the flies dropping from the papers on to the piles of food freshly taken out from the electric stove.

- THE FRONT ROOM -

Of all the rooms in my grandmothers house the front room held the greatest fascination for me. It had a presence and atmosphere hallowed with the time and long occupancy. It was a warm room where my grandmother sat in her old arm chair by the fireside, her mind full of memories of her long life. There were two memories which dominated the latter years of her life; both of them sad.

It was on a scorching hot August day in 1936, that she heard the news that her husband Charlie had been killed in the quarry at Stepper point where he was the foreman. He had been home for lunch with gran and Aunty Kath. He had kissed her goodbye and returned to his afternoon work as usual and less than an hour later he was dead. It was a neighbour and close family friend, Joe Wills, who brought the tragic news that he had been hurled over the cliff after being struck by a truck which had not been properly fastened higher up the incline of the quarry. He fell some seventy feet to his death. It could so nearly have been a double tragedy as his younger son Eddie, who was working with him, had been knocked to safety by the same truck. The coroners inquest conducted a few days later with evidence given by fellow quarry men and by Doctor Shirvell, the family doctor, stated that death was due to a fracture of the skull, lacerations to the back and multiple injuries. He was the third fatality at the quarry. Some two years earlier his brother-in-law Wilfred Gilbert, husband of his youngest sister Ida had met his death there.

The August of 1936 had been hot and dry with only just over half an inch of rain recorded in Padstow and it was one of the beautiful cloudless days of that month when the funeral took place at the Church of the Good Shepherd. The coffin was taken to a tiny little church through the sash window and only the immediate family were able to mourn within the church. Many stood outside joining in the service.

The hymn was aptly chosen, 'God moves in a mysterious way'. I can picture the large congregation singing, 'The bud may have a bitter taste, but sweet will be the flower'. The bud was indeed bitter but the flower of my grandmother's faith sustained her in those dark days. The service was conducted by a son of Padstow, the Revd. Ewart Worsley, who was home in Padstow for the August holiday.

After the service in the church the cortege proceeded the two and a half miles to Padstow Cemetery. In front of the coffin walked the manager of the Quarry Nr, J.A. Atkins and the forty one employees there. He had been a popular man there and this token of appreciation was their way of showing sympathy for the family. A walking funeral was a great occasion in a small community.

It was in this same room on a dark winters day in December 1944 that she heard of the death of her elder son Arnold. The Christmas decorations were still around the room for Christmas was barely over. My mother had received the dreaded brown envelope with the telegram in on Christmas Eve. She had kept the news from my father's family until Christmas was over. This was a typically unselfish action on her part. My mother had been through a difficult time when the Prince of Wales was sunk earlier in the war but then he was one of the survivors. H.M.S. Aldenham had been lost off Corfu on the 14th December 1944, my father perishing with the ship. How long and how sad Christmas must have seemed that year. How difficult each succeeding Christmas must have been for her but she made the best of it for me. Her grief was deep and the scars of her bereavement never fully healed for Arnold was the only love of her life from the time she stayed at Cove as a young teenager.

My mother bore the hurt of loneliness and I suspect some degree of bitterness in silence. For years she could not bear to have a photograph of my father around. I only recently learnt that was because I had a habit of hiding under the dining room table and looking up at my father's photo on the wall saying, 'I can see you but you can't see me'. She knew only too well that he could not see the wife he loved and the son he idolised. These words bore deep into her heart like the stabbing of a sharp knife and so she removed the picture. After moving from Hawkers Cove to Padstow the photo re-appeared.

'La la Gran' was small in stature but large of heart and there was a quiet dignity which age and experience had given her. Life had been hard but her suffering had defined her personality. She sat for hours in her old armchair by the fire reading the Daily Herald, Christian Herald or a letter from one of her children with whom she maintained a regular correspondence. She would read aloud from the paper which she usually read from cover to cover. It was the tragedies, sadnesses and hurts of life which drew her comments. I can still remember her reading a book about a fire which killed several children and hear her quiet voice saying 'poor lambs, poor lambs' for she knew what it was like to lose a son, who was undoubtedly her particular favourite. She had reared her seven children strictly but her grandchildren knew her only as a gentle old lady with rounded shoulders and a mass of beautiful silver hair.

Her presence then graced the room but it was the table which dominated it. The oval gate- legged table which was usually covered with a green cloth when not in use and a snowy white cloth at meal times. The table was then laden with all kinds of Cornish fare. Sunday tea time was a great family occasion. Her house was usually crowded as she loved people. Families and relatives enjoyed visiting the Cove, to see her and to sample her delicious cooking.

Hers was not the only presence in the room, there was Aunty Kath, her unmarried daughter. Aunty Kath was short and dumpy with one leg smaller than the other. She had a TB knee when she was sixteen. It was originally diagnosed as Housemaid Knee but as it grew worse she was sent to Plymouth Hospital and Tehidy Hospital which was for TB patients. Eventually the knee cap had been removed. Consequently she walked with a dot and carry movement. Her disability did not limit her life. She had a tremendous zest for life and a wicked sense of humour not usually found in spinster ladies. She had brought home her numerous boyfriends to this room and never married any of them. She was kind but bossy. Bossiness being one of the traits of the family. Perhaps it was because many of the family were short. When she was approaching sixty she rode pillion on a motor bike with her short leg sticking out at a forty five degree angle to the bike. She even ran a little when encouraged by Cynthia, one of her nieces. This brought her near to tears for she did not realise that this was possible. She rowed her yellow punt, the Saucy Sue with vigour and would anchor it off shore as she listened to her wind-up portable gramophone which she carried with her in the boat or when the family went to the beach for picnics.

There were four beautiful high-backed chairs which belonged to the table, they were graceful and added to the presence of the room. When not in use they were placed either under the table or against the walls of the room.

On the east wall of the room adjoining the passage was an old Victorian piano. The piano was like a large altar or shrine for on the top of it were numerous photographs of the family. Her husband Charles in the uniform he wore during the First World War and all her grand children in various stages of childhood. The portrait of her mother and father however, hung in her small, cold, north facing bedroom. She was devoted to her tall bearded father who I, as a child, thought looked like one of the Old Testament figures which I saw in her old bible. She loved her gentle and diminutive mother.

The photographs were of all shapes and sizes, framed and un-framed, many of them school photos then in only in black and white. She was particularly proud and fiercely protective of her grand children. On the lid of the piano were numerous old hymns and on the music stand were many pieces of sheet music, mainly the hits of the immediate post war years. You had to move the books to play the piano which she loved. She was very much the product of Victorian piety. She loved you to play a 'Sankey' hymn from the green covered Moody and Sankey 750 pieces. Her children had been raised in this

'Aunty Kath' Kinsman

religious school where emotion played such a large part. She loved the sugary harmonies and the tear-jerking words of these hymns which told of dying children, returning penitents and, above all, of a land that is fairer than day. But for all that she was no humbug, she firmly believed in what she sung in her sweet alto voice. Until her dying day, each night, she would pray the prayer which she said through all her life. Indeed at the times when she suffered one of the many strokes she endured, words of prayer would be on her lips.

The piano had candlesticks attached to it but there were never candles in the holders. I would swirl them round wondering why our own piano did not have them. The keys were yellow with age and one or two of them were cracked but this did not deter members of the family from playing the piano. On Sunday evening the family gathered around it to sing hymns. Firm favourites included 'Dare to be a Daniel', 'Beulah Land' and 'Let Your Lower Lights Be Burning'. The family sang with enthusiasm and zest, they never did anything by half measures. Gran would sit in her chair and sing the alto part while the fire smoked in the chimney, and smoke it did, often filling the small front room with fumes! Certain directions of wind caused billows of smoke to puff out into the room.

The fireplace situated in the corner adjacent to the kitchen wall was a Victorian one but the surround had been painted by Aunty Kath. The scene portrayed was one of Corfu near to where my father's ship was lost. She had copied this from the Geographical magazines which she loved to read. It was her memorial to him. My father had been a great favourite with his five sisters and with his mother.

Over the fireplace was the mantlepiece where numerous articles of bric-a-brac were to be found gathering dust from the fire. Two of the most prominent were a lady dressed in blue with a parasol and a gentleman wearing knickerbockers. The only photograph on the mantle was one of my father in his naval uniform. There was also a small plaque of the Papal Holy Year 1932-33 given to the family by the Breton fishermen. Above the mantle was the clock which ticked the hours away. The pendulum was visible through the glass face and the clock was surmounted by a horse. It struck the hours and half hours in this house of routine.

Arnold Kinsmen

The midday meal was always at 12.30pm. My aunt would blow her whistle to summon her nieces and nephews who often stayed there to dinner. Two blasts on the whistle meant come and eat and woe betide any of us who were late for the meal.

Afternoon tea was at four o'clock, but it was no ordinary tea, particularly on Sundays. It was a Cornish tea 'par excellence' with every square inch of the table covered with various kinds of food. Large Cornish pasties with the ends hanging over the plates, some made of potato and meat, some potatoes, onion and meat, some potato, beef and parsley and two rather different kinds on occasions, a turnip and butter pasty which Gran herself liked and a squab pasty which had apple, mutton and spice as its ingredients. The meat in these pasties were real pasty meat not the minced variety as today is often found in 'boughten traad'. Egg, bacon and parsley tart which was delicious - how yellow the eggs seemed then. Potato cake cut into squares sometimes eaten hot and sometimes cold, rather indigestible but delicious. Apple tarts always served with the inside of the pastry facing upwards and the outside of the crust facing the plate to which was added the cream made from scalded milk. I always thought the cups of tea tasted strange with scalded milk in. Another favourite was sweet egg custard tart with sultanas and currants and lemon peel in. There was usually a jelly or blancmange on the table for tea.

The proximity of the sea meant that all kinds of shellfish were served. Crabs, especially the meat from the legs, either in sandwiches or in a dish to eat with a tomato and lettuce. There was usually a dish of cucumber very thinly sliced and well soaked in vinegar which we were told helped digestion. Lobsters and crayfish, when in season, were eaten. Shrimps and prawns often caught by the family in the gigantic shrimping net in the passage for use usually on the Bar as we called Doom Bar. Cockles and mussels were sometimes eaten. The children picked mussels off the rocks below the cottages while the cockles came from the bar where you went cockling. Although Sunday tea time was the highlight of the week it had already been preceded by a roast Sunday dinner. Sunday was not Sunday without a proper roast dinner. We never called it lunch. When Gran's family were young it was often pork from their own pigs

If there was none Grandad Kinsman would row to Padstow and fetch a joint of beef or lamb from Butcher Hawkins.

During the week there was always a hot meal every day. Some time ago one of my fathers sisters Lena talked of the meals she had as a child. At one point she began to smile and chuckle 'we often had leek pie but after Aunty Kath told her that the leek looked like snob', she never ate it again. The Kinsmans have weak stomachs and are easily put off their food by comments such as these.

Often the main meal of the day would be a fish dish. I can remember opening the back door and being greeted by the smell of fish sizzling in the large frying pan on the electric stove. Gran made the most delicious fish cakes using ray, which my Londoner Gran called skate. Herrings, mackerel, plaice, sole, ray, pollock and haddock were all cooked and enjoyed. The herring and mackerel were often 'soused' in vinegar and cloves with bay leaf added. These were particularly tasty when eaten cold.

The most popular 'afters' were milk puddings, none of which I liked. My mother rarely made them but Gran made them frequently extolling the virtue of drinking much milk. I found the texture of the puddings unpalatable although no doubt they were delicious.

I was a very faddy child. My mother must have had great difficulty in feeding me on her very limited income. She enjoyed the rice, sago and tapioca puddings which Gran and Aunty Kath made. Certain milk puddings were always referred to as frogs spawn.

My mother particularly enjoyed junket with nutmeg on the top, but, like my father, I did not. This was often made for Sunday tea along with jellies and blancmanges. Gran's jellies had fresh orange or lemon juice in.

At Christmas she made a really dark Christmas cake, ingredients of the cake included brandy which the Breton crabbers gave the family in return for some of her homemade cooking especially pasties. Although brought up in a teetotal home and signing the pledge she did not think it inconsistent to make homemade wines especially potato wine, sloe wine and blackberry wine. I rather suspect she learnt this art from her mother-in-law. The Christmas cake was baked for hours until it looked really dark and then later it was marzipaned, iced and decorated. Among the decorations were hard, edible, silver balls. Often the Christmas cake lasted well into the New Year and the longer it was kept the harder the icing became. You took a risk with your fillings if it was being eaten in February.

I liked her rich yellow saffron cake with fruit in the best. This was another Christmas speciality. It had real saffron in and you could see the stamen of the plant in the mixture as she made it up. Saffron was expensive and bought by the dram. No wonder any expensive purchase was said to be as dear as saffron. She also made a white or yeast cake at the same time. The large earthenware bowls were left to plum before being cooked.

Some weeks before Christmas the Christmas puddings were made with a remarkable number of ingredients including chopped nuts and stout or guiness! These were boiled in the copper and the kitchen seemed full of steam on these occasions. Gran Wells also made her own Christmas puddings and these had silver threepence bits in them which I eagerly sought to obtain for my coin collection. She made an iced Christmas cake But it was far less dark than the Cornish variety. My busy mother often iced her cake after finishing work on Christmas Eve at midday.

My mother was essentially a career woman who learnt her cooking after she was married and never really liked house work. She was, however, a very good cook and could make a beautiful pasty despite not being Cornish by birth. I am sure that she became Cornish by adoption for she played quite an important part in the life of the town at Padstow.

The fire in the front room at Cove had a fender around the small hearth and on the fire was the brandis on which sat the kettle. There was always water in the kettle which was only just off the boil so that with great speed a visitor could be served a hot cup of tea. Tea was always drunk in large cups which I heard described on one occasion as breakfast cups. I have never seen such huge cups anywhere else.

The rest of the furniture in the room included two armchairs, one by the fire which was Grans and the other on the west wall of the room which I loved to sit in disturbing the cushions or disarranging the embroidered arm pieces. I once dared to put my foot on the armchair. My mother scowled at me hoping I would desist before Aunty Kath saw. Gran noticed and said nothing. Her own children would have been thrashed for such audacity.

The sofa belonged to Aunty Kath. This was her seat and it was positioned under the window almost resting against the wide window ledge. She had spent hours lying on it when she had been ill and this was where she rested after dinner while listening to Radio Athlone and the after dinner music programme. The old wireless stood on the cabinet between the sofa and the door to the passage. In winter two thick brown curtains were hung across the two doors in the room. We as children hid behind them and sometimes caused angry comment when we shut them in the door. The door into the passage was not used in winter by the adults but we used it if we wanted to aggravate Aunty Kath.

The particular favourite of the children was an old portable gramaphone which lived behind the sofa. If supervised by Aunty Kath we could play it. The spring had to be wound before each record was played, great care was taken not to over wind it. The records, mainly ten inch 78 records, were kept in the cabinet under the wireless. There were also some old twelve inch records which had recordings on one side only. I loved to listen to the gramophone and became familiar with the hits of the 1930's and 1940's which formed the bulk of the records. The really old records included one of the great Italian Tenor Caruso sing 'La Donne est Mobile'. While the gramophone played Aunty Kath would sing to the music and swing her short leg which always stuck out from the sofa in time to the record. This leg intrigued me but it also puzzled me. When I asked my mother what was wrong with Aunty Kath's leg she explained why the leg was as it was but told me not to ask her too much about it. Her knee cap took a great time to heal but she swore that she healed it with the use of peroxide which was used by the family to clean up any wounds which looked at all suspect. The sensation of the peroxide fizzing and bubbling in a cut was one of the familiar feelings of my childhood.

When I was about eight, one of the old gramophones which my Aunt had, was reconditioned and given to me. I could then play records of my own. One record which my Grandad Wells gave me was 'Aint it grand to be blooming well dead'. Whenever I visited Padstow cemetery with one of the family the words of that record haunted me especially the phrase 'Look at the tombstone I'll be a pancake'. I don't think Gran Kinsman approved of my singing this song.

The chiffonier, which was probably quite valuable, occupied the west wall adjacent to the window with its wide ledge. The chiffonier was like a sideboard but it had an ornamental top on it. The cutlery was kept in the drawer, and in the lower part which had two doors in it were the condiments and sauces. The glass cruet sat on a stand with four sections in it for pepper, salt, vinegar and mustard. The vinegar was often clouded and had small pieces of sediment floating in the glass bottle. These were referred to as 'mother'. I loved vinegar as a child and smothered the salads with it. Often when my mother was at work I would have my tea there before she returned home. She would always leave my tea as she could not expect Gran and Aunty Kath to provide it. My mother was fiercely independent and did not want to be beholden to her in-laws and their families. Despite this they related very well and Gran and Aunty Kath loved my mother, often saying she was a good wife for Arnold and she was a wonderful mother to me, which she undoubtedly was. In the summer this tea was salad. There was always extra cakes and buns which I particularly liked made by Aunty Kath.

As a child I rarely drank tea and so there were Corona drinks including Dandelion and Burdock, fizzy lemon and fizzy orange. Aunty Kath would encourage me to drink lemon barley which she drank in quantities for her kidneys. She had some kind of kidney problem.

It was very difficult to open the right hand door of the chiffonier and impossible to open the left hand door as it was wedged against the end of the sofa. The HP sauce was on the cupboard section and I loved this with the cold pasty which was often part of my tea after returning from school. Often I would be told that I should not put so much sauce on my pasty as it spoilt the flavour.

Behind the sofa were bottles of home-made wine. Blackberry wine, elderberry wine and potato wine. My grandmother made these, she had learnt the art of this from her mother-in-law Harriet Kinsman.

It was these home-made wines which were responsible for an amusing incident at my parents' wedding! The reception for the wedding was held in the Legion Hut in Padstow. Gran did not want the children who attended the reception to have sherry or any other alcoholic drinks so she provided home made wines for children. The result being that her eldest grandchildren and youngest nieces and nephews were rather drunk.

In the large window ledge were all kinds of plants including geraniums. Aunty Kath kept her atlas and stamp collection there. We were allowed to look at the collection if we were good. In the evenings she would spend time looking at the collection and checking the countries of origin from the atlas. She loved geography but disliked history. She knew the rivers and capes of Great Britain and could recite them. The geography she learnt was the kind prevalent in the early years of the century where note learning played such a large part in a child's education.

The view from the front room window was magnificent. In the foreground was the last of the Lifeboat house built in 1931 with the adjacent wooden landing stage. Beyond was Hay Field and Tregirls Cove. Battery Point, Rock and Tregirls Farm marked the limits of this panoramic view. The lifeboat mechanic lodged with Gran and Aunty Kath for many years after separating from his wife. He tied his fishing nets to the large legs of the table when mending them. He was the first person I saw with an electric razor. This fascinated me when I watched him shave. He was a kind man with a happy disposition but also a very good lifeboatman with a thorough knowledge of the sea. Aunty Kath had a deep relationship with him which was never discussed openly in front of us children. On Sunday afternoons Aunty Kath and he would retire upstairs to work on the books. I never knew what the books were but they must have been particularly interesting to them as this happened every Sunday.

Family parties were held in the front room when all the children were at home. My aunt Lena remembers the girls dancing with each other while Will French played his accordion. The gate-legged table was then pushed back to the side of the room. I can remember at least twelve to fifteen being there on family occasions. The noise in the room was deafening as the Kinsmans were great talkers, hearty laughs, and at their best when the room was full of family. The network of the extended family was so much greater then. Great-grandparent Hooper always had lodgers and guests at Trevear. Joseph Hooper's Aunt Jane Brokenshire ended her days there as did Mary Hooper's Uncle James Udy. Jane was a stern and foreboding spinster and James a saddened widower who had buried all his children before his death. Great-grandparents Kinsman in their very small cottage reared their nine children but also had Harriet's mother Mary Champion and blind sister Mary Jane living with them for some time. My own grandparents, Charlie and Lydia began their married life in the tiny cottage where Dorothy their eldest daughter was born. How they all slept in a minute two-bedroomed cottage one can never imagine. Despite very hard lives with many tragedies loneliness was hardly known, for here was a large and supportive family at times of bereavement and hardships to share in the hurt and anguish. The front room of the house invited guests, it was as if the family was fulfiled by the presence of other people. They loved entertaining and giving to other people. Hospitality was natural to them for there was a graciousness and real love for people in their very bones. In material terms they were not rich but it was in this room I experienced a different kind of richness which is very hard to put into words. There was a deep and enduring warmth. You were made to feel wanted and of value by the family. The love which I had from my mother and Grandparents Wells was centred on me as I was an only child and grandchild. The love I had from Gran and Aunty Kath was no less real but was shared with all of her large family. Gran rarely talked to me about my father but when she did you could see the deep love she had for him and also the grief and inner sadness which she bore with dignity after his death. The Victorians found it easier to deal with death than we do today.

This room epitomised home to all of her children and grandchildren and indeed was the favourite place for the visits of her numerous nieces who loved to see Aunty Lyd and her family. I thank God that this room wove its spell on me and that I have a real and enduring bond with all members of the Kinsman family.

The pantry was a minute room but it served as more than a pantry. You entered it through a door from the kitchen or the small dark passage leading to the front door. It was full of all kinds of objects including a mangle and a copper. The copper was used for boiling clothes which were invariably washed on Mondays. The mangle was ancient and you turned the handle to wring the clothes dry. It was great fun to turn the handle but after a short time it became hard work. Modern washing machines and spin driers have lightened the load of the housewife. In those days washing took a whole day and often if the weather was consistently wet the clothes took several days to dry.

There were certain superstitions associated with washing. My grandmother would never wash blankets during the month of May for she said to do so was to wash one of the family away. She would never wash her front door step on New Years Day. I am not certain of the reason for that. The family had other superstitions which were probably common to many Cornish people. You never looked at the new moon through glass. It was important to go outside to see it. If you wore glasses it meant taking them off before gazing at the tiny crescent shaped moon. The appearance of a single magpie meant something sad or even disastrous might happen to you for did not the old rhyme say 'one for sorrow'? Two, however, were a good sign, heralding 'joy or mirth'. It was rare to see more than two magpies. The fishermen from Hawkers Cove would not sail out to sea if they saw a rabbit playing on the cliff edge fields. It was even worse if you happened to see a parson on the shore when embarking or sailing your boat.

By the mangle was a marble top on which were placed a bowl, usually full of soapy water, and a bar of soap and a flannel. You were expected to wash your hands before each meal in cold water. The only hot water came from the kettle boiled on the electric stove in the kitchen. Behind the door to the passage there was a roller towel. If you only dipped you hands in the water and wiped them on the towel the dirt would be transferred to the towel which you moved around leaving only a clean piece of towel for Aunty Kath to see. One day I was asked if I had washed my hands to which I foolishly replied 'look at the towel and you will see'. On occasions we rolled the towel around at high speeds.

The pantry was a very cold room and, like most of the house, extremely draughty. The window looked out to the north and when a northerly gale blew up the estuary this room was like an ice box. This made it a suitable place to keep food. There was always a jug of milk covered with a muslin cloth weighted with small beads to secure it firmly from flies. Flies were a constant menace in the house. The cold meat was kept in a safe hanging on the wall with a perforated zinc door. Along the wall which divided the kitchen from the pantry was an open dresser with shelves containing cups, plates and dishes used in the house. There were some Coronation mugs hanging on the hooks amongst them. The mugs commemorated various Coronations, King George VI in 1937, King George V in 1910 and the oldest of them, King Edward VII, in 1902. There was also a Silver Jubilee mug of George V from 1935.

The mugs were proud possessions as Gran and Aunty Kath and indeed the whole family were ardent Royalists. Gran would read all the references to the Royal Family in the newspapers with great interest and suitable deference. At the end of her life when there was a black and white television at Cove one of her greatest joys was to watch state events like the Trooping of the Colour. There was a deep and instinctive bond between ordinary people and royalty. I remember being taken to Wadebridge and standing with my mother and some other relatives at the top of West Hill to see King George VI and Queen Elizabeth driven by while on a visit to this part of Cornwall. This was, I believe, in 1950. It was a wonderful moment when Queen Elizabeth (now the Queen Mother) raised her hand and waved regally in the very special way that she does. How proud Gran would have been when I was presented to Prince Charles during his visit to the Royal Cornwall show in 1984 when I was in charge of the pastoral work for the Cornwall Council of Churches Tent. I was very impressed by his manner in dealing with people but also surprised how short he is.

Aunty Kath built a small cement sink on the window ledge and a cold tap was installed over it. This must have been at some point in the 1950's and for the first time there was running water indoors. Previously it had been collected from a tap on the cement or from the large rain water tank outside the front room window. Our own Coastguard house had indoor water for as long as I could remember. Indeed we had a bath which was covered in by a large table top when not in use in the back kitchen. It must have been somewhat of an achievement to build this little sink for she had no training for that kind of work although she possessed the native practical skill of the Kinsmans and also their determination.

Under the marble wash stand was a small cupboard of even two cupboards. In these were kept bottles of Corona which were bought from the Corona man who called every fortnight selling his wares. There were bottles of still orange and lemon barley. The lemon barley was an important part of Aunty Kaths life as she had some form of kidney problem which the doctor diagnosed as pyelitis. Dr. Sheldon pressed her to drink vast quantities of lemon barley which she dutifully did. The doctor was an authority figure and his words were hung on to and acted on with alacrity. She also had little white crystals presented by him and kept in a large round medicine bottle with a brownish tinge and a screw top and wide neck. These when placed in a cup of water fizzed merrily. I often wondered what this effervescing drink tasted like, she let me have a sip or two, the taste was not unpleasant.

At the end of her life when she was diabetic and had a heart problem she would have to take up to twenty tablets a day and she unwisely mixed them up in a large jar or container. We were all very concerned about her having the tablets indiscriminately mixed in this way. On one of his visits Dr. Gay, the then senior partner of the Padstow practice, warned her about the danger of this. She recounted his warning to my mother and me on one of our weekly visits to her during the latter years at Hawkers Cove. 'The doctor told me that I should not do this' she testily told us. We asked her what she said to the doctor. 'I told him that I wasn't stupid'.

There were also a number of fizzy Corona drinks in bottles with a china type top with wires attached, these were a form of spring used to keep the top secure so that the drink did not loose its effervescence and become flat. Aunty Kath enjoyed the visits of the Corona men who were usually younger than most of her visitors. She drank a great deal of fizzy Corona, one of her particular favourites being Dandelion and Burdock. I preferred the ' fizzy ginger beer'. This was not my favourite ginger beer. Grandad Wells sometimes bought a bottle of Schweppes 'Ginger Beer' which was infinitely superior in taste. This was a special treat for me. We sometimes bought a bottle of this on the train while travelling to London on the Atlantic Coast Express. There was a refreshment bar on the trains built to look like a miniature public house bar. It was called the Green Man and sold alcoholic and non-alcoholic drinks.

The pantry, like the kitchen, had beautiful old beams in which, on hooks, were hung the pieces of salted pig. They remained there a reminder of the years when the family kept pigs.

- THE PASSAGE -

The pantry door lead into the passage which was always extremely dark except when the front door was open. There was of course no window there. The stairs ran parallel to the narrow passage from opposite the front door. It was separated from the stairs by the banister on which we slid when not being in danger of being caught by Aunty Kath. The staircase was wide with a carpet runner placed in the middle while the slides of the treads were painted. The staircase had a small landing about two thirds of the way up. This was often the site of the commode which was used by Gran and Aunty Kath particularly when they grew too old to walk to the lavatories on the edge of the cliff. At other times the commode was placed on the upstairs landing or in one of the spare bedrooms. The commode always smelt strongly of dettol.

I was not frightened of the darkness of the passage which was surprising for I was a timid and sensitive child with a vivid imagination. I loved the darkness especially when the sky was lit up with the innumerable stars twinkling light years away from Earth. The Cornish air has a particular clarity and is at its best in a North Westerly airstream following a period of rain. The stars talked to me of other worlds and green men particularly when I became an avid reader of the Eagle which had a serial where green men from other planets appeared.

The most beautiful sight of all was a full moon over the river. The Harvest and Hunters Moon of autumn lit up the Doom Bar giving it a supernatural quality. It was hard to believe that on this Bar hundreds of ships had been wrecked. Autumn is more than a 'season of mists and mellow fruitfulness' it is the precursor of winter, a time to be enjoyed before the wet and stormy days of winter take over. The joys of autumn are intense but short lived. There is an impermanence about which matches the restless moods of the Kinsman family which I have inherited. We as a family are capable of great intensity in our relationships with others but on the whole need to be valued for what we are. We expect from others a deep and whole hearted response and are hurt if we do not receive it.

There was an occasion when I was very frightened by a different kind of darkness which was far less benign than that I experienced at Hawkers Cove. I felt the full horror of a London smog while staying at Hornchurch with my Grandparents Wells. The occasion is still vivid in my mind. We had been visiting relatives and it was either just before or after Christmas. While we had been there a real peassouper of a fog had descended silently and menacingly. The first indication of this was when we opened the front door of the house where we had been to be met by the evil and acid smell of smog. The world was still, sound being muffled by the blanket of acrid smoke. We had a long walk to the nearest underground station. It was difficult to see even your hands or the face of the person nearest you. The walk was a nightmare to me, I was thankful I could clasp the hands of my grandparents who walked each side of me as we slowly and diffidently walked to the nearest station. The smog was evil and menacing and seemed to personify the powers of darkness. Was this a foretaste of Hell with its sulphuric powers?

The Jehovah Witnesses had visited our house at Cove and described in detail what the end of the world would be like. Had it arrived, I wondered? It was easy to dismiss their message on a warm summers day with my mother standing close by. She readily countered their assumption that they would be the only people to survive this cataclysmic event. I have always felt that it was immoral to preach sermons which frightened people into believing in a God of love. I have never preached a sermon about Hell although I have never experienced in my darkest moments the sense of total alienation from God and from others which an absence of love can bring.

Immediately on the left inside the passage was a door into the coal house. Coal was delivered to Cove by Bray and Parkyn's lorry from Padstow. Each sack of coal was carried from the road by the coalman on his back. It was a good two hundred metres. The men had to hump the sacks one by one. The coal was ordered in the summer when the price was at its cheapest and also when the weather was often at it hottest. By the time the coalman had delivered the whole of the order he was bathed in sweat and must have been totally exhausted. The last part of the delivery journey was difficult as it meant coming through the kitchen and pantry of this meticulously tended house and tipping it into the sheer darkness of the coalhouse. Paper was placed on the floor to minimise the dust which settled there. When the poor man had finished his Herculean task he was rewarded with a strong cup of tea and a yeast bun or piece or cake.

The coal house contained not only coal but also a small pot which we as children used to pee in. This pot was also used by the adults particularly in bad weather. It was emptied into the long gully drain on the cement outside the back door. The cats also had their kittens in the coal house. There was a candle holder with a candle in and some matches there. The light of the candle was an aid to assist you in peeing straight. It was easier for us boys than for the girls to use it in those dark and cramped surroundings. A large bottle of dettol was also kept in the pantry. Dettol was used to keep the pot fresh and clean but also used to bathe a bleeding knee. How often as children we seemed to have scabs on our knees from falling over. How great was the temptation to pick off a scab before it was ready to come off naturally. Picking scabs or picking your nose were considered not the done thing. It was even worse if you picked your nose and flipped the snob or 'snot' at another person. My mother preferred to call the mucus 'a bogey'.

The boot and shoe polishes and brushes were also kept in the coal house which consequently had an overpowering smell of polish, dettol, coal and pee which gave it an unforgettable odour of its own.

The sticks for lighting the fire were also kept in the coal house as were the garden tools and clippers used in the front garden. There were also tins of paint.

Along the wall of the passage adjoining the front room was the bench which had formerly been used by the family when the seven children were small and it had stood in the kitchen. It was little used by this time but could be carried out into the front garden if so desired. On the wall above the bench was an old aneroid barometer which was regarded by the family as an accurate method of forecasting the weather. "The barometer's falling, we shall have some rain and wind", was a familiar cry. We all tapped the barometer to see if it was going up or down. As I became more and more interested in the weather and as I studied climatology as part of my A level geography course I realised that barometers should not be tapped. I can remember telling Aunty Kath that she should not tap the barometer. I deserved the reply I received -. 'All right Mr. Know-all Kinsmen', she retorted. She was most accurate in her assessment as we as a family have the tendency to think we know all there is to be known about everything. This was particularly true of me as a child and a teenager. As I grew older I realise more and more how little I know and how short is a single life to acquire a fraction of the knowledge which I would love to possess.

A small stand attached to the wall at about eye level held two telescopes, one of which was in much better condition than the other. These were little used as it was the binoculars kept in the front room which kept constant surveyal of the surrounding countryside. It was difficult to focus the telescope correctly.

On the same wall was a mirror and a brush set which were little used but reminded us all that originally the front door was used by those coming by boat at Hawkers Cove. My grandmother took in paying guests during the summer. They were wonderfully looked after and came year after year to stay. It was by boat from Padstow that my Grandparents Wells and my mother came first in 1924 to holiday. My mother told of the excitement of the journey by boat from Padstow Quay to Hawkers Cove. The kindly good nature of Charles Kinsman was soon revealed to them as they travelled by boat and saw for the first time one of the finest views there could possibly be. The main channel at that time was still on the West Side of the estuary. I expect Charlie pointed out the various landmarks of this sea journey. The North Pier at Padstow was not yet built but on entering the boat they would look back at the old town of Padstow quietly dominated by the ancient tower of the Parish Church of St. Petroc. Behind the town were the arc of trees circling and enfolding the grey stone houses of my beloved Padstow. The best view of the town is that seen by boat entering the harbour. The ferry coming from Rock has a privileged vantage point.

The only houses above the old town were those on the West side of Dennis Road with the Dinas Hotel beyond, which is now the Dinas Nursing Home. The London and South Western Hotel, later the Metropole, which was built to accommodate the influx of visitors following the opening of the railway in 1899, was then experiencing the many distinguished guests including King Edward VIII, then Prince of Wales. There were also a number of the large houses in Station Road. The rest of the rapidly growing 'up town' of Padstow was not even a dream in an architect's mind.

Charles would have pointed out the newly erected Granite War Memorial at St. Samsons Point which was the memorial to those who were killed in the First World War. It also commemorates those who gave War service to the country and returned. He could little have thought that there would be another World War and that his elder son Arnold's name would be added to those who gave their lives for King and country. There can be few War Memorials with such a splendid view. It stands on the site of the medieval chapel of St. Saviour built probably for sailors to give them thanks in after returning home from sea voyages.

On Remembrance Sunday following a service in the Parish Church, the parade of Servicemen and Women, the Royal British Legion, and other uniformed organisations marched there to lay their wreaths. When I was a choirboy the service was always held in the afternoon at three o'clock. In the church were sung the traditional hymns associated with that sad and solemn day. It was a very special day in our house. My mother found it very difficult, she could never face the Remembrance Service although on occasions she attended Evensong. She watched or listened to the Act of Remembrance held at Cenotaph in the morning. This was in the safety and seclusion of her home when she could be alone with her deepest and most personal emotions.

The Remembrance Service was a highly charged experience for those who had lost loved ones in the war. I was never far from tears as the huge congregation sang the hymn 'O Valiant Hearts' of heard the sound of Reveille or Last Post echoing through the huge parish church. As I grew up I thought that my deep emotions would become less and they appeared to until on one Remembrance Sunday when I was teaching at Didcot in my first teaching post. Following the Parish Communion at Northbourne Parish Church there was a short act of Remembrance at the War Memorial in the churchyard. It was on this occasion while acting as crucifer that suddenly to my embarrassment I was in tears, the tears were streaming down my face and I was totally unable to control the deep seated emotion of the moment. I had a similar experience on a totally different occasion. This was following the presentation made to me on leaving Hooe Junior School at Plymstock where I had three of the happiest years of my life. The presentation was over and I returned to my classroom and sat at my desk only to be convulsed with a deep paroxysm of crying. I just could not stop.

The conduct of a funeral often brings me momentarily to tears. I always find it a deep experience. The preparation of an address at a funeral is time consuming and draining. I think it is because you are probably closer to people at a time like this and you have within you the power to give them support at the most vulnerable time of their life. I hate to have to conduct the funeral of a person I do not know for I can not speak with authority about them. I feel that to speak with sympathy and empathy involves having ministered in some depth to the family and the deceased.

To return to the sea journey from Padstow to Cove, Charlie Kinsman would have pointed out the beautiful cove at St. George's Well where legend has it that St. George landed. He would have shown the newly arrived guests the two small buildings on the beach which were used for changing in. One of them belonging to the Prideaux-Brune family.

The house on Battery Point where the Thomas family lived was still standing. When the boat came to this point Hawker's Cove came fully into view. He was nearing home and the new guests were fast approaching a house that was to become a second home to them. The Wells family loved their holidays at Cove. They looked forward for fifty weeks to this fortnight's holiday there. The boat soon arrived at Hawkers Cove and they were helped ashore climbing up the rocks from the water. The front gate of Number Four Hawkers Cove led into the south facing garden and finally up the three slate steps by the front door into the passage. What a warm welcome they received. Gran Kinsman had met Jim Wells when he stayed at Trevear Farm some fifteen years before. There were still at least five of the children at home. My mother, an only child, soon became a firm friend of the girls and also in due course of Arnold.

Gran and Grandad Wells slept in the four-poster bed in the front room while my mother shared a bed with some of the girls in the girls bedroom at the back of the house.

Behind the front door was a curtained form of cupboard and on the other side by the door to the front room was a huge heavy surf board. The board was carried great distances by the family when they surfed either at Trevone or Harlyn Bay. Tregirls Beach, the nearest beach, was sheltered and within the estuary so that it was no good for surfing. I have, however, seen the waves in a particularly bad storm break over Battery Point. The cliffs were then much higher than they are today.

- BEDROOMS -

The house had four small bedrooms or, more technically, three bedrooms and a small box room. As you came to the top of the stairs there was the box room facing south looking out on to the small cove in front of the house. There was a sizeable gap between the stairs and the entrance to the box room. Aunty Kath, whose bedroom it was, negotiated the gap with skill. This small room was jam-packed with furniture. The small single bed was placed across the window so that she could lie in bed and look out at the Cove and also see the road which led to Hawkers Cove from Padstow. She was, therefore, able to see the arrival of cars late at night and also to look at the cottage where she had first lived at Hawkers Cove. For a number of years her sister, Beat, and brother in law, Fred, and niece, Cynthia, lived in the cottage. She knew from her vantage point their movements and especially what time of the night they went to bed.

What a wonderful experience to lie in bed on a warm summer's night with the window ajar, and the gentle sea breeze just disturbing the curtains, and the sky full of stars, with, perhaps, the moon giving added light and reflecting on the waves lapping on the slipway of the Arab house. The rise and fall of the tide each day added to the rhythm of this orderly house. It was exciting in winter when the cove assumed a totally different mood. The sound of ground sea roaring on the Doom Bar formed a background to the swish and send of the pebbles being tossed to and fro by the angry waves. The waves would break with ferocity on the rocks below the house while the wind lashed with tremendous force on the small window panes. The rain usually found its way onto the window ledge as the window did not fit properly. There was an inner security lying in bed in this house, it was as if the storm of life, which had been many for the Kinsman family, had not succeeded in shaking their deep faith.

It must have been draughty sleeping so near to the window but the view compensated for that small discomfort. On the east wall of the bedroom was a smallish wardrobe which contained Aunty Kath's clothes, many of which she made herself as she was a skilled needle-woman. There was a sloping wooden area above the stairs where she kept her books. Many of them were second- hand school books which, I believe, came from Dr. Lord who ran a private school in the Long Room area behind the Ship Inn in Padstow. Aunty Kath knew the Lord family. She used these books when she acted as a kind of tutor to two mentally disturbed girls called Rampling who lived in Treverbyn at Padstow... Her essential kindness would have made her a very suitable person for this onerous position. By the side of the wardrobe was a jug and basin set, which were used for washing. All of the bedrooms had these sets. What a laborious task it must have been to fill them up when guests stayed in the house. On the wall hung an old cuckoo-clock which never worked in my childhood. 'Why doesn't your clock work Aunty? 'I would like to see the cuckoo come out.' I asked, but it never did. On a small table beside the bed was the candlestick, or was it the night light? Probably the latter. Aunty Kath always kept a torch under her pillow before the electricity was installed in the bedrooms.

Directly opposite was the bedroom which had been the girls' when they were small. In early days the two boys had slept in the box room.

The girls room faced north and in consequence was very much colder than the box room and the front bedroom which were south facing. There was an old iron double bedstead with its head against the east wall. A wardrobe was placed across the corner of the room and a jug and basin set stood on the wash stand just inside the door. But it was the large picture of Daniel in the Lions Den which dominated the room. It stood on the wall above the wash stand. Daniel in the Lions Den was a favourite story with grandmother's generation. They were not troubled by the fact that the story was written to illustrate that God was preserving the Jewish people during the time of their persecution by the Hellenistic groups in the Second Century BC. They had not heard of modern Biblical Criticism. They fervently believed in a God who looked after those who put their trust in them. The miracle of the preservation of Daniel after his night in the den of lions was ample proof of God's care for His own. The lions had a very ferocious look which added to the impact of the picture. Daniel was prepared to stand alone for his principles which was enough for my grandmother with the Hoopers blood readily flowing through her veins.

The window looked out onto the back garden which was reached by crossing the gulley which ran the length of the cement and climbing a few steep steps to the garden level. The garden was almost level with the middle of the downstairs windows.

The boys had jumped out of the windows onto the garden when put to bed in disgrace. It was a good method of escape. I doubt whether Daniel watching from the wall would have approved of this, but the girls did as they watched this happening quietly suppressing their excited giggles as they watched from the iron bedstead.

The other north facing bedroom was that of Gran Kinsman. It was small, cold and somewhat draughty with an iron bedstead in it which was later replaced by a modern single bed as she became older and more infirm. I can picture her sitting up in bed with her old-fashioned flannelette nightie on and wearing a blue bed jacket. She looked so serene and gentle as she lay there, as if all the passion of her life was spent. When she was ill, as she often was during the last few years of her life, she rarely complained. There is a gracious dignity about old age which she possessed.

The bed was in such a position that she could look across to Daymer Bay and almost see Donathan, where her father had been born. She could also see the Greenaway Rocks, where the Padstow Lifeboat Disaster of 1900 took place. Many a time during the long period she lived at Cove she had seen the lifeboatmen return after being at sea for hours searching for, or standing by, a vessel in distress. While the Lifeboat Mechanic lodged with the family each trip took on an added importance.

I have a very personal and special picture of Gran Kinsman kneeling beside her bed saying her prayers before getting into bed each night. The prayers seemed to go on for such a long time. Prayer was an important part of her life. My aunts recall her father , Joseph Hooper, praying so loudly that they could hear him in the garden. He was very deaf towards the end of his life. My aunts were somewhat amused by the volume and intensity of his prayer. His loud cries upon God were accompanied by a pounding on the wall. His hands were thumping on the wall to emphasise his earnest religion of that evangelical kind demanded great fervour but often missed the still, small voice and knew little of the sacramental life of the Christian.

In the latter years of her life she used as one of her prayers the following prayer:

Lord, grant me strength to do the task that every day demands,
Give me faith and hope, a happy heart and willing hands,
Be thou close to me O Lord and hear me when I call,
Light a star above my path when twilight shadows fall,
Help me to accept whatever comes with every day,
And if I should meet with trials and troubles, this I pray,
Lead me by the quiet waters of tranquillity,
Where my soul shall find its comfort and its peace in Thee.

The quiet waters of tranquillity of her latter years were only arrived at through the many trials and troubles of her life. In the twilight years of her life she lit within her grandchildren a star, which still shines brightly, of a lovely old lady whose faith sustained her through all the changes and chances of this mortal life.

There was the usual washstand and basin in the room and the portraits of her mother and father hung over her bed on the west wall. I wondered why she did not sleep in the warmer front bedroom but it was only at the very end of her life, when she was partly paralysed after a series of strokes, that she moved into the room. By the side of her bed was often a jar of humbugs which she particularly liked and often some boiled sweets with nuts in, another favourite of hers. These made her cough. She had a very distinctive cough which appeared to come from her throat. As a small child I imagined that her best coat with a velvet collar caused her to cough. I hated the feel of velvet.

The front bedroom was the largest and it was the room where the guests stayed. It had a magnificent four poster bed with curtains around. I would love to know where it came from but have been unable to find out. The bed had a feather tie on it and so it was a very comfortable bed to sleep in. My grandparents Wells slept in it when they stayed each year at Cove. The bed had an east-west-orientation and when in bed you could look out of the south-facing window at the beach and sea below. By the side of the bed was a large dressing table with three oval-shaped mirrors. It was fascinating to look at yourself at three different angles if you moved the mirror. There was a large wardrobe on the east wall. This was the only bedroom with a fireplace, although I can never remember a fire being lit in it. The chimney was above the fireplace in the front room. By the side of the fireplace was the customary washstand and basin set. There was also a commode which had a beautiful silver cushion on the top. I never remember it being used although I assume that guests must have used it. The best things in the house were reserved for the guests who in turn became family friends. You could never stay here without becoming part of my grandmother's family. She loved all the people who came and was somewhat in awe of them. The family always imagined that people who came from London must have a considerable amount of money. I think my grandmother and Aunty Kath always thought my grandparents Wells were well off. Although he worked hard in his office job in the city they had to save hard to pay off the mortgage on their bungalow.

In front of the window was a large comfortable arm chair which gave one a commanding view of the Cove. In the window-ledge, which was usually bathed in sunshine, there were seed potatoes placed on sheets of newspaper. These were no doubt removed when people stayed.

- PIGHOUSE GARDEN, CLOSETS AND WATCH HOUSE -

One section of the garden faced Brae Hill and Daymer Bay. This was known as Pighouse piece. It was a large strip of garden which was used in my grandfather's day to grow vegetables, mainly potatoes, which formed an essential part of the diet of a large family then. At the bottom of the garden and of the other Pilots gardens which ran parallel to this were the pigstys and other small houses which contained the bucket closets.

These houses were stone built with a door usually painted black, or in one or two cases, green. They faced the sea and the pigstys were at the rear of the buildings.

It was a long, cold and often windy walk from the Pilot Houses to the closets, probably the distance of at least 100 metres. Inside the building was the large toilet seat with a big hole in the middle, the hole on the top of the seat had to be lifted to insert the bucket or remove it to empty when necessary. The inside walls were whitewashed and behind the door hung squares of newspaper which were later joined by rough toilet paper. Soft toilet paper was not in use in homes when I was a child. The toilet paper was Izal which my grandmother believed killed all germs. It was fascinating to read the squares of newspaper but disappointing that a spicy story was continued on another sheet which had already been used. The squares were part of the Sunday People, Sunday Graphic and, I believe, the Sunday Pictorial, the papers which my grandmother bought on that day. They were joined by her daily paper the Daily Herald. My grandmother read the Daily Herald faithfully each day and voted Labour in the 1945 and 1950 elections although coming from a Liberal background. Her weekly paper, the Christian Herald, was never placed in the toilet as it was not thought seemly to do so.

My grandmother never really approved of my mother allowing me to read all the papers. She was concerned about what I might read and indeed did read. On Sunday afternoon when we visited Gran along with many other members of the family I would pick up the papers and read far more than she ever realised. Human nature does not change, and the Victorians, of which she was one, had a great fear of the effect of reading about fallen human nature. Today the foibles of humanity are blazed across the T.V. screens into every home in the land. My mother did not believe that I could be wrapped in cotton wool and totally protected from the reality of the world. I am grateful that I had such a broad minded mother and that I am not easily shocked. This has been of great help in my ministry.

The human sewage from the bucket closets was tipped over the cliff at a certain point beyond the three houses. Each house was semi-detached with a toilet in each section. At this point the path narrowed and there was a gap in the bushes which grew between the path and the sea cliff. You could tell you were approaching this particular spot by the smell, and the collection of pieces of newspaper and toilet paper which appeared to grow on the bushes. Each day my aunt would 'empt over the cliff' the slop pail from indoors and when necessary the bucket from the toilet. The slop pail had a strong smell of dettol. On one occasion I had the tenacity to say that I didn't think that this procedure was very clean - her reply was terse but laced with humour. 'It is food for the fishes'.

Behind the closets were the pigstys where, at one time, all the Pilots kept pigs. It was considered good management to have a pig who could eat up all the scraps and left overs from the table and provide a good source of meat when salted for the family. Pigs were a great stand-by for cottagers who, it was said, ate all but the squeal. This was often the only meat which they ate. My grandmother, being a farmer's daughter, was a great meat eater and beside the pork which came from the pig, my grandfather would row to Padstow and buy a joint from Butcher Hawkins for the Sunday roast.

Mr. Baker and my grandfather killed the pig and this was a great event. The pig was cut up into pieces which were hung up on hooks in the pantry beams after being salted for future use. These hooks were still in the beams when I was a child but the days of pig keeping were over. The family kept three or four pigs when all the children were at home and my grandmother made hogs puddings and brown from the pigs remains. As a farmer's daughter she knew how to use all the parts of the pigs to make tasty and varied meals. Nothing was ever wasted. On the table in the pantry there was always numerous small dishes with the remains of various meals for future use. The remains of Sunday joints and vegetables were used up for Monday's dinner which was often 'bubble and squeak'.

The family would tell a delightful story about a pupil of Padstow School who was late for afternoon school. Mr. Crapp, the Headmaster of the boys' school, asked the boy, John Thomas, who later became a very successful Headmaster - why he was late. 'Please, Sir, my father had to annihilate the pig'.

The path beyond the little house led to the Watch House which was erected by the Padstow Harbour Association and commanded a view of Stepper Point, Pentire Head and the mouth of the estuary from the North Window and of the Doom Bar and the main channel from the East Window. At one time some form of bad weather or permanent watch must have been maintained as the house had a little fireplace in it and a hard wooden bench. John Baker used it to store crab pots in the years following the Second World War.

The house once had a resident for short and intermittend periods, Sammy Fielding. Sammy was one of the great characters of Padstow Mythology. He was a Sea Cook who loved Padstow May Day and would walk from the nearest port of embarkation for the great day. He once walked all the way from Liverpool or I believe strictly Birkenhead. His favourite expression 'Heave the bugger overboard' was used frequently if anyone displeased him particularly when he was inebriated. He would sleep on the hard bench in the Watchhouse and to keep warm he lit a fire in the chimney there. He would appear and disappear at random. The children of Hawkers Cove would tiptoe to the door of the Watchhouse to see Sammy asleep on the hard wooden bench. Life was much rougher in the early years of the century but characters more apparent. I have often speculated why we have fewer real characters today. I heard it once said that the coming of universal education was responsible for this but I believe it has more to do with the pace of life and the sheer greed of the age in which we live where the ability to make money is the criterion of success. Many of the great characters were financially poor but had a philosophy of life which was basically non-conformist and individualistic in outlook.

~ THE FAMILY ~

I have briefly mentioned the family but now I think that it is time to introduce them all to you and see how they fitted in to the small community at Hawkers Cove. Let me begin with my father, William Arnold Joseph Kinsmen (1909-44). Arnold, or "Arnie"as he was always known, was the elder son and fourth child of William Charles and Lydia Jane Kinsman. (NB. The Registrar recorded my father's surname as Kinsmen but the family name is Kinsman). He was born at Trevisker Farm which is situated just off the main A 389 road from Padstow to Highlanes. My grandfather at that time worked as a farm labourer there. Arnold was a smallish, good-looking man with a tremendous sense of humour which revealed itself in the numerous childhood pranks which he played on the family. He was dark,with hair which had a tendency to curl and thick bushy eyebrows like many of the family. After leaving Padstow School he entered the Royal Navy and had risen to be rank of Chief Stoker before he was lost off Corfu when the H.M.S. Aldenham was sunk on December 14th, 1944. In his youth he had been a great favourite with his family and numerous friends. He loved Cove where he came as a baby in arms and where he was christened in the Church of the Good Shepherd. His interests were tap-dancing, at which he was quite accomplished, boxing and fishing. He had always loved the sea so his desire to enter the Royal Navy was not surprising. He was interested in machinery and engineering and was very good with his hands. In all senses he was a practical man. I have not inherited these qualities.

His mother Lydia was devoted to her son whose impish sense of humour allowed him to get away with various forms of bad behaviour which she would not tolerate in her other children. He was the child who burnt my grandmother's cane as it hung on the mantelpiece in the kitchen ready to be used whenever a child spoke at meal time. He was the child who jumped down the cliff after being chased by his irate mother. There was a special relationship between them. After he was killed Gran never played the piano again, it was as if music had gone out of her soul.

I have only a few memories of my father for I was only just over four years of age when he was killed. I can, however, remember being hoisted on to his shoulder and carried about around the small courtyard outside our house in the Coastguard Station at Cove. I can also remember seeing him in the Naval uniform, either at the beginning of a spell of leave from his ship or was it prior to his returning to his ship? These are the only definite memories of the man whose facial characteristics I have inherited. I have often thought about which of my traits have come from him besides being very like him in appearance. I am not practical as he was, my love of reading and the ability to communicate came from the Wells family.

I think that I owe to him two most important characteristics. First, a strong, well developed and at times wicked sense of humour. My mother had a much drier sense of fun. Secondly, a love of people which means that I am never happier than when I am with a crowd of friends or relations.

My mother was much more of a loner but she, like my father, was a very kind and generous person. His sense of rhythm and music has been conveyed to me and I am perhaps most like my father on Padstow May Day when I follow the 'Obby Oss' around the streets helping with the singing and even teasing the Oss. My love of May Day has led to certain of my clerical friends dubbing me 'The Pagan Parson' and suggesting that it is not quite proper for a priest to prance around with the Obby Oss which is, after all, a pagan fertility symbol. I have never regarded my love of May Day as incompatible with my priesthood. That town, indeed one of my ancestors, Thomas Trevethan, was a Port Reeve there in the reign of Elizabeth I. His name is recorded in the Court Leet of the town. The Court Leet was a manorial Court dealing with petty offenses such as common nuisances, highway or ditch disrepair and breaking the Assize of Bread and Ale. The indictable offenses went to the Assizes. It was presided over by the Lord or his steward. Every man over the age of 12 in some places and 16 in others, with a residence of a year and a day, was obliged to attend although in practice it was only the main tenants. Although it appears to have met more frequently in Padstow, the Court met, in theory, twice a year, and as well as considering allegations of offenses, elected various officers including the Reeve. The word reeve means a deputy. He was usually a man of villein status elected by his fellow tenants to organise the daily business of the manor.

This often made him responsible for speaking for the manor in negotiation with the Lord or his steward. He received a manor payment from the villagers and sometimes a remission of rent and a remission of feudal dues.

The Court Leet at Padstow met normally in April and again in late September or early October. There were several references to the Trevethan family. One of the earliest is from the reign of Henry VIII in 1539 when Thomas Trevethan is among those in debt, probably not paying his contribution to the Reeve's expenses. At the same Court Leet, held on the Friday after Michaelmas 1539, George Trevythaven is noted among the Free Tenants. The same Thomas became Reeve in 1558 at the end of the reign of Mary I, however, he did not carry out his office to the satisfaction of other tenants and was presented to the Court for allowing the little pigs of the inhabitants of the borough to run at large against the law and custom of the Town. He was fined 3/4d. Pigs wandering around were the biggest nuisance on manorial land. They often scavenged food from other people and even in some areas rooted out bodies from the churchyard. He was again Reeve in 1570 where he is described as Thomas Trevythan gentleman. This did not stop him being involved in a foray which ended with him being presented some two years before the Court for assaulting, beating, wounding and drawing the blood of John and William, sons of Peter William.

Padstow was a very lively place at this time and the Court rolls are full of cases of assaults. In 1554 William Carne, an Irishman, alias Longwell, with others, assaulted the Bailiff. The same gentleman and his wife Elizabeth were in court in 1561 for assaulting Ralph Burlace the Constable of the Parish while exercising his office. Many of the cases refer to people taking pigs from the pound or penfold which was situated in High Street which was once known as Pound Lane. In 1559 George Carter, labourer, assaulted the bailiff and carried off two stray pigs which he had taken to the penfold, while in 1563 John Lane Jnr. son of John Layne, a free tenant of the Manor broke the penfold of the Lord and took out some sheep of his - put there and impounded by David Nicholls. This was done without licence from the Reeve.

A number of cases refer to non-observance of the assise of bread or the assise of ale. These were jealously guarded in every borough with the loaf weighing a pound and the ale being one pint. In 1554 Dinorisisus Layne was fined 6d for not keeping the assise of bread and Richard Dagell and William Vyan for not observing the assise of ale.

The wreck of the sea belonged in part to the Lord of the Manor and in 1563 John Newton lately at Lalyseek (Lelizzick) found a soyle (seal) and did not let the Manor know and so was presented to the Court.

It was then, in this tight knit community of Elizabethan Padstow that my ancestors, the Trevethans, lived and were obviously much involved in the community.

We need to return to my father after this digression. He enjoyed a short but happy marriage. He was the only love of my mother's life for she had known him since she first stayed with the Kinsmans at Hawkers Cove. Jim and May Wells, her parents first came to Cove in 1924, when my mother was nearly 13. They fell in love with the little community and it became their annual place of holiday from then until Grandad Wells retired and they came to live in Padstow in 1951.

There was, however, an earlier connection between the two families. Jim Wells worked at Samuel Hanson's in Eastcheap in London. Here he was joined by Arnold Hooper, Gran Kinsmans brother. They became firm friends and in 1909, the year before Jim Wells married, he came to stay with Arnold Hoopers parents at Trevear Farm, St. Issey where they farmed. Jim never lost touch with the Hooper family. During that holiday he first met Charlie and Lydia Kinsman so the introduction was made to the Kinsman family. Grandad Wells travelled quite widely in this area and he loved it. He often told of attending Evensong at Little Petherick Church and the fact that there was no sermon at that service which particularly pleased him. The Kinsman family were kind people, not highly educated but with a

Arnold Kinsmen

certain native intelligence and a very earthy sense of humour. They came originally from the South Hill and Callington parishes in East Cornwall. My great, great grandfather, William Kinsman (1840-1895), was the child of Elizabeth Kinsman, conceived like so many, out of wedlock. I have never been able to find out if she eventually married. She is a figure of mystery, a young woman of twenty when he was born, but thereafter just the name on a census return of 1841. I am pretty certain that William's birth was never registered. Was it shame or ignorance which prevented this?

William moved to the St. Neot area where he met his wife Caroline (nee Trevethan) (1840-1880). He served his time as a journeyman mason and was, I believe, a skilled and practical worker. Caroline and he were married at Liskeard Register Office in 1863. His wife was the daughter of John and Joanna Trevethan. John was a miner who moved from Blackwater near Chacewater but then in the parish of Kenwyn to East Taphouse in St. Pinnock Parish. Many miners moved eastwards when copper and tin slumped in the 1850's. He brought with him Joanna (nee Whitford), his young wife, and at least two children. Caroline worked with him at the mine, for she was a bal maiden, one of the women who worked on the surface where the ores were refined. She, like so many who worked in the tin and copper mining industry, contracted 'phitisis'. She was only 40 when she died of that dread disease. Her death certificate records this fact and states that she had been two years with it. There had been a tradition in the family that T.B had been the cause of her death. Those last two years must have been tragic for she left William with six sons under the age of seventeen to bring up. Their only daughter had died in infancy. All I know of Caroline is that she had a fine singing voice which was in much demand at Tredinnick Methodist Church in St. Neot Parish where she sang solos. It was said that her voice could be heard at Ley, a small hamlet some half a mile away as the crow flies. I can picture her struggling to sing as she had always done but being totally unable to do so as her lungs rotted away filled with the dust of the mines.

After her death, William travelled abroad and became a stranger to his own family. Older members of the family have told me that on his return to Ley his own children failed to recognise him even throwing stones at this apparent stranger. He returned to Cornwall before his death, dying in Plymouth Hospital of cancer of the gall bladder. I have the bill for his funeral which included making his coffin and for carriage to Connon Methodist Chapel.

He, like Caroline, is buried in Connon Methodist Chapel Cemetery. The music in Caroline's veins passed to John Kinsman (1863-1941) their eldest son. John, or Jack as he was always known was short, slight man with brown eyes who worked for most of his life as a farm labourer at Treveigo Farm in St.

Winnow parish near Lostwithiel. His wife, Harriet, was a Champion from Ley village. John was a great cowman who went to Smithfield with the cattle, even sleeping with them as he prepared them for the show. Jack played a concertina and obviously enjoyed music. He was a quiet man with a basic good nature. At the time of his marriage to Harriet he worked as a labourer in the railway maintaining the track that carried the main Plymouth-Penzance line through the beautiful Glynn Valley. He, like his father, was married at Liskeard Register Office. Harriet (nee Champion) (1863-1937) was a large buxom woman with a mischievous sense of humour. She had fleshy arms and ample bosoms. She loved life and people and was considered to be a great character. She was earthy but warm-hearted. Her father Thomas John Champion (1820-1897) is said to have fathered over 20 children. His wife Mary (1816-1910) came from gypsy stock for she was a Crocker. Mary was small and wiry with sight in only one eye , for she, like John, had been injured in an explosion at the powder mills at Twowatersfoot, near to the present Trago Mills, where they both worked. John lost both of his arms in the accident and had a yolk which could be fitted to his shoulders enabling him to carry goods and water from the well to his home at Ley.

Sometime after Jack and Harriet's marriage they moved to Lower Coombe in St. Winnow Parish. The eldest members of their family, including my grandfather William Charles Kinsman (1883-1936), were born at Ley. Jack and Harriet's cottage at Coombe was an isolated one with no access by road and could only be reached by crossing fields and descending a steepish slope to where the cottage was built by the side of a stream. It has not been occupied for many years and now only a few remains can be seen.

In that little cottage she reared her nine children, cooking delicious meals in the cloam oven, making homemade wines, tending her geraniums and other plants which she loved and collecting all kinds of bric a brac and ornaments. The little cottage was always full of people and laughter. She was a perfectly

Wedding of Arnold Kinsmen* and Winnifred Wells, 7th December 1935, at Padstow Parish Church

natural woman who accepted people as they were. There was no pride in her character for she was totally happy in her home surrounded by her family and visited by her friends. Her children and grandchildren loved this plump, jolly, motherly figure. They knew however, that she was very likely to play all kinds of practical jokes on them. Her humour was not malicious but was inspired by her great capacity for affection.

Jack and Harriet's life was hard. They had a crippled daughter, Elsie, who lived at home with them until her death at the age of 42. She had jet black hair as did their youngest daughter Ida. Most of the Kinsman family are dark like Elsie and Ida. Jabez, their second son was lost at the battle of Jutland in 1916 and Claude the youngest son was gassed during the first world war returning home a spent force with his lungs permanently damaged to live for a few more years as a pale shadow of his former self. Claude was, by all accounts, a smart, kind and warm hearted man. Claude and Jabez' portraits hung in the kitchen of number four Pilot Cottages. They were both photographed in their naval uniforms.

After leaving Lower Coombe, Jack and Harriet moved to Fairy Cross (Sandylake) to a cottage on the main Lostwithiel to Liskeard road about a mile and a half from the former town. They loved their roadside cottage and would often sit outside looking across the valley towards Restormel Castle or watching the traffic passing by. By now Harriet's health was indifferent, she was overweight with high blood pressure.

They were yet to experience another cruel blow, when my grandfather, their last surviving son was killed in August 1936.

Within nine months Harriet was dead, the victim of a heart attack. Jack then went to live at Redlake, also in St. Winnow Parish. He lived with Florrie, one of his daughters, and her husband, Charlie Mutton. Jack died in 1941 and, like Harriet, he lies buried in St. Nectan's Church quite near to Lower Coombe where they lived happily for much of their married life. Great Aunt Florrie was very much like her father, small, kind, gentle with dark brown eyes. Her kidney was encased in silver, the result of suffering from some kind of ailment when young, it could have been T.B. I remember being told this as a child and feeling decidedly queasy when I next ate a steak and kidney pie. It was from her that I learnt some of the family history which related to the Kinsman family. Great Aunt Florrie was by then living with her daughter and family at Fowey. It was a slow but beautiful journey from Padstow to Fowey by train, it involved a change at Bodmin Road, now called Bodmin Parkway, and at Lostwithiel, finally taking the attractive river side branch to Fowey. Most of this route is now closed with only the main line remaining. Florrie had the family sense of humour and would recall incidents and people who then became part of my life. One of her most vivid memories was of the visit of George, her father Jack's youngest brother. He was a soldier who arrived at Coombe smartly dressed in his red uniform with brightly polished silver buttons.

William Charles (Charlie) Kinsman was Jack and Harriet's eldest son. He was a well built man, broad shouldered with a tendency in middle age towards plumpness. His demeanour was quiet and kind but he could on rare occasions show a very fiery temper. He, like his father, was a farm labourer for most of his early life. He was only 19 when he married his wife Lydia Jane (nee Hooper) who was four years his senior. It was a happy marriage although Lydia was undoubtedly the boss. One of the occasions when the family saw his anger was when he returned from work to find that one of his daughters had been kept in at school by Miss Angove. The other members of the family had returned home without her. He did not stop to eat his tea but strode off in high dudgeon to Padstow School. He entered the classroom without knocking, picked up his daughter, telling Miss Angove that he, Mr Charles Kinsman, was taking his daughter home. The normally strict teacher was totally non-plussed and in his words as related to the family after 'she couldn't blow nor strike'. This true story is a reminder that quietly spoken and apparently gentle people can be very angry and determined when really upset.

The Hooper family were not too pleased when Lydia, the daughter of a farmer, married Charlie who was a farm labourer. The Hoopers were proud, with a certain degree of pretension. They would have been even more disturbed to learn that Charlie's grandmother Mary Champion (nee Crocker) had been of gypsy stock. They were married at Bodmin Register Office and lived with the Kinsmans at Coombe for the early months of their marriage. Dorothy, their eldest daughter was born there.

Soon after her birth they moved, and for the next seven years moved often to places such as the Lizard, St. Merryn, Tregingey in Little Petherick Parish and Trevisker in Padstow Parish, where my father was born. They moved only once after this, to Hawkers Cove in 1910.

Charlie rarely showed his temper in his relationship with his wife Lydia. Lydia was very short and thin when young with a tremendous capacity for work. She was like very short people, extremely determined. She had originally been dark but by the time she was thirty her hair was already the beautiful silver colour it remained to the end of her life. Her hair was soft, silky and quite distinctive.

I called Gran Kinsman 'La la Gran' because she sat me on her knee singing to me and rocking me up and down singing 'la, la, la'. My mother's mother was May Gran because her name was May having been born in that month. Both of my grandmothers were wonderfully kind to me.

Lydia was the third child of Joseph and Mary Wood Hooper (nee Trevethan) and was born at Trevance, St. Issey, in March 1880. Her father had a small shop at that time. His occupation is described as shopkeeper on her birth certificate and 'huckster' in the Baptism Register of St. Issey Church.

The Hooper family were a total contrast to the Kinsman family. They were proud and ambitious people who sought to advance themselves, very set in their ways and decidedly prickly in their relationships. Lydia brought up her seven children very strictly, perhaps she needed to. She was the mistress in her own household though devoted to her easy going husband whom she dominated. There was in her make up an outward puritanism which did not reflect her gentle heart.

Joseph & Mary Wood Hooper, my great-grandparents

Her father Joseph Hooper (1844-1931), was a tall man over six feet in height, as were his three brothers. He had decided views and a touch of hypocrisy in his outlook. He was born in St. Minver Parish at Donathan, a farm next to St. Enodoc Church now called Penmain. His father George (1806-60) was a farm labourer there. The Hoopers were an old St. Minver family being in the parish from at least the Seventeenth Century. Joseph's mother, Sarah, was a farmer's daughter from St. Winnow Parish (Lostwithiel) where her father, Joseph Brokenshire, lived. The Brokenshires had originated in Roche parish.

The photograph of Joseph shows him as an almost patriarchal figure with a flowing beard. His lips are thin and his eyes rather small but very determined. He was a dominant person whose family lived in awe of him. When Dennis, my father's eldest sister's son was born, Joseph saw the infant and exclaimed "Don't praise the child, but his Maker". Joseph remembered until extreme old age entering the partly buried St. Enodoc Church through the roof. Family tradition had it that he read the lesson at the Church but this is highly unlikely as his background was that of a farm labourer's son. St. Enodoc Church was a Mediaeval Chapel of ease to St. Minver Church. Joseph, the youngest of the family, was only sixteen when his father died and he was then working as a shepherd. He later became a farm labourer, possibly on the farm of Thomas Trevethan (1791-1880) who farmed Great Keiro at St. Minver. Mary Wood Trevethan, his eldest granddaughter, kept house for her widower grand-father and it was then Joseph Hooper met her. Joseph and Mary were married at St. Mabyn Methodist Church in 1875. Mary Wood Hooper was a little lady, meticulous in appearance, quiet of speech, and very much under Joseph's thumb. She had a gentle sense of humour and a warm and loving heart. She would always find a word of encouragement for her family. Her childhood had been very difficult for she was the eldest of the thirteen children of Thomas Trevethan (1825-1901) and Nancy (nee Udy) (1825-1898). Thomas was arrogant and opinionated and bore the nickname 'Rumbump-

~Paternal Grandprents~

Lydia Kinsman　　　　　　　　*Charlie Kinsman*

tious'. He was a farmer whose philandering was well known in St. Issey Parish. He had a long and scandalous relationship with Elizabeth Veale who, it was said, he seduced by climbing in through the dairy window of Trevear Farm where his son-in-law, Joseph, later farmed.

As a result of this very public scandal all of Nancy's brothers emigrated to Australia but they never lost touch with their mother and sisters. One of them, William, who became a prison Governor in Australia returned to England on a visit in 1924 when he had a cornish granite cross erected in St. Issey Churchyard 'In memory of Thomas and Nancy Trevethan' bearing the words 'erected to all Trevethans and Udys resting in foreign parts and at Home'!

The principal sufferer of Thomas's wayward relationship was his gentle and long suffering wife, Nancy, who did not deserve such a randy husband. Nancy was a devout Bible Christian, a ticket holder of Burgois Chapel. Nancy was a member of the Udy family, who were typical products of the Evangelical awakening brought to Cornwall by John Wesley. They were hardworking, sincere, warm and anxious for others to share with them 'in the saving power of Christ'. Their faith was no cant or humbug. My grandmother, Lydia, had a great respect for her mother's cousin James Udy, the blacksmith evangelist who was born at Pleasant Streams, St. Issey, later moving to St. Erth where he had the village forge and blacksmiths. The Udys were of mining and farming stock. James Udy like John Wesley felt that he was a 'brand plucked out of the fire'. As he watched the fire in his smithy he felt the call to preach to others. He earnestly desired that others might have the same joy he found in his deep faith. The

Udys were always of a missionary nature. James numbers among his descendants a number of Methodist Ministers and Anglican Clergy.

The Trevethans and Udys were two of the oldest families in St. Issey Parish. The Trevethans living in the parish from the beginning of the Eighteenth Century and the Udys since at least late Mediaeval times when John Udy was Vicar of St. Issey in 1440.

The Trevethans came from St. Merryn and Padstow parish originally.

~ THE CHURCH OF THE GOOD SHEPHERD ~

One of the most important buildings at Hawkers Cove was the galvanised covered Mission Church of the Good Shepherd. It began its life soon after the building of the Coastguard Station. It was in March 1902 that the first plans were conceived to build a School and Mission Room to serve the small community. The Revd E. F. Nugent who was the Vicar at the time was an energetic and devoted incumbent. He was a typical product of the Anglo-Catholic School of the Anglican Church. He firmly believed in the sacramental Life of the Church, and the Eucharist was celebrated daily at Padstow Church while the offices of Matins and Evensong were publicly recited daily. He placed great importance on visiting and teaching. It was his deep concern for the children at Hawkers Cove which led him to encourage the building of the School and Mission Room. The Padstow Parish Magazine which has appeared for over a hundred years records in its issue of March 1902 that "through the kindness of the Lords of the Admiralty and C. G. Prideaux-Brune Esq., the Vicar has been enabled to erect a little room as a Sunday School and Mission Room for the use of the Coastguards and Pilots and their children. Both have contributed £25 towards it ... The Vicar will be very thankful to receive further help towards furnishing the room with necessary things. He proposes to hold a little service one evening in the week, and a little Sunday School and, moreover, a lady resident has been good enough to volunteer to hold a little private school there on weekdays for the little children who find it almost impossible to walk to Padstow. It was in that March, actually on the 18th, that the Bishop of Truro, who had been Confirming at the Parish Church on the previous night, accompanied by the Revd. E. F. Nugent walked to Cove to see the newly erected building.

The tiny Church was built by a Padstow builder, Mr. Harry Champion, and was opened in Easter week of that year. We read of this in the May Edition of the Parish Magazine. "On Wednesday afternoon the new little Mission and School Room at Cove was formally opened and the Coastguards had made it very bright with flags and both Coastguards and Pilots rendered much assistance." Miss Chapman, daughter of the farmer at Lellizzick, had previously held Sunday School in the cottage close by. Miss Witham, who came from Trevone, shared with her in the preparation of an excellent tea on this occasion. Miss Witham ran the day school in the building for which the pupils paid a 1d a week. She also gave a tea to the children of Cove on the evening of the 26th of November of that year. "About twenty-eight children sat down to tea."

Sadly, Miss Witham left the area in August 1903, and, on the departure of the Revd. E. F. Nugent to the living of St. Martin's, Brighton, in July of that year, services ceased and were only resumed in the December when the Revd. W. C. Thompson became Vicar. The services were resumed and held "except when the weather is so stormy as to prevent the Clergy walking out." This was the practice for many years and services were often intermittent, ceasing whenever the living was vacant or there was no Curate in the Parish. The stipendiary Lay Reader who conducted the services at Cove when I was a child either walked or rode his bicycle to conduct the Friday evening service. In 1908 The Church Army Mission Van visited Cove from the 6th to the 10th March as a part of a Mission to the rural section of the Parish.

The Harvest Thanksgiving Service was already the highlight of the year. The service of 1909 was typical "It was held on Sunday 10th October at 3pm. The magazine notes that the room was exceedingly well decorated and quite full of worshippers. The Vicar the Revd. E. Williamson preached the sermon."

One of the novelties of the Edwardian period was the Magic Lantern and this was used as part of a series of Lantern Services held on Tuesday evenings in the following year. It was in 1910 that the Little Room was enlarged and a small iron chancel with altar made by one of the local shipwrights, Mr. Cocks, was added. A porch was also erected at the South-West corner. This was the final form of the little Mission Church.

After the enlarging of the Church, Holy Communion was occasionally celebrated and, when the Parish had a Curate, often on a monthly basis. Services were held for many years on a Sunday afternoon. The pattern was, Sunday School at 3.30pm followed by Evensong at 4pm. The Church remained open, with short intervals, until part way through the Second World War.

Mr. and Mrs.William Capell were two of the most indefatible workers for Cove Church. He was a Lay Reader and conducted the Evensong for many years and his wife assisted with the Sunday School. They walked in all weathers from Padstow to minister to the congregation at Cove. After the service they were entertained to tea by one of the families, Congregations grew, and the highlight of the year, as already mentioned, was the Harvest Evensong for which the Church was beautifully decorated. Around the walls of the church were hung fish nets, often with real fish in them. Sprigs of blackberries were used to add variety to the decorations. As a child I stood on the seat of the pew and ate some during the service, much to the chagrin of some and the amusement of others. My family reminded me of that incident when I first conducted services there after being licensed as a Reader in March 1965.

Dahlias and Chrysanthemums and other autumn flowers from the beautifully tended gardens of the Cove lent a richness to the building. The small oil lamps on the walls glowed through the decorations, while the numerous candles in the sanctuary and on the altar lit up the Church. Around the Archway of the sanctuary was the inscription 'In hoc signo vincet' - "In this sign conquer." These words were not fully understood by the Congregation but they knew that the words were in Latin and that they were particularly important. The brass candlesticks, of which there were many, shone, reflecting hours of loving labour spent in keeping the Church spotlessly clean and well cared for.

Miss Bessie French spent hours cleaning the Church, polishing the brass and washing the altar linen. Bessie was the daughter of Orson and Ellen French, who lived next door to the family for many years. I remember her as an elderly lady living in one of the Alms houses in Padstow. I often visited her little home with her great nephew Michael Barr, who was a childhood friend of mine but sadly died at the age of 13 from Polio. Bessie's Almshouse was spotless, with everything in its place spick and span. It needed no imagination to see why Cove Church was so beautifully clean when she lived there.

At Christmas-tide in Pre-War days the Parish Church Choir would walk to Hawkers Cove to sing Carols in the Church. The sound must have been magnificent, as the Choir was a very fine one with many outstanding voices. In the latter years of the Church the Padstow Carollers would sing on the Friday evening after Christmas for the Annual Carol Service. The Church was absolutely full then, with people standing at the back and in the porch. When Cove was full of young families in Pre-War days, Con-gregations at Harvest Festivals and on special occasions were large. When the evenings were light or if it was an afternoon service the sash windows of the Church would be raised and the overflow congre-gation would sit in the small grassed area between the Church and the stone wall of the field.

The Church was raised off the ground at the sanctuary end and, in consequence, you could climb, or, more exactly, wriggle under the Church there. I never fancied this as you came out covered with dust and small pieces of twigs and dead leaves. Ants lived there in profusion, too.

It was, then, in this small Mission Church that I learnt the rudiments of the same Christian faith that St. Samson and St. Petroc brought to this area so long ago. This faith was to play such a significant part in my life. The Mission church had been closed at some point during the Second World War but it was re-opened in 1949 while I still lived at Hawkers Cove. The services were, for the most part, conducted by a Welshman, David Griffiths by name, who was the Stipendiary Lay Reader of the Parish. He cycled or, occasionally, walked the three miles from Padstow in all weathers to conduct Evensong which was held on a Friday evening at 6.00pm. He had a strong Welsh accent with many idiosyncratic pronunciations of words which as a young child intrigued me. The strangest, but by far the most amusing, was the way in which he pronounced the phrase in the Apostles Creed 'He ascended into Heaven', which he rendered as 'He arse-ended into Heaven', filling the pious yet precocious child with horror.

There were his Sermons which he read quickly often showing that he did not really understand what he was reading. It was said that he had bought them or even inherited them from a long deceased Vicar. We did not mind because he was a kind man who visited us in our homes and showed a real interest in the little community.

His first wife was much older than he. She was a large and very straight-laced lady who was shocked by one of my comments. I was by then about twelve years of age and living in Padstow and a choirboy at the Parish Church (from where, my Mother said, I learned all the news and gossip of the town). One particular Sunday evening Mrs. Griffiths was telling a group of women including my Mother, with me hovering in the background, that the RAF Chaplain's Wife had just bought a baby. She was careful not to say that his wife had given birth to a child. This was not seemly in front of a young boy. I was puzzled by this and exclaimed 'Do you mean that they have adopted a child?' I wondered why an icy silence ensued. My mother was amused and often told this story to her friends. I had not been brought up with stories about storks, or children being found under gooseberry bushes, for my questions about the facts of life had been truthfully answered.

Cove Church was lit by small oil lamps which hung on the walls, the heating being paraffin stoves placed in the aisle at strategic points. The Service was Evensong according to the Book of Common Prayer - it never varied. The small congregation knew exactly what to expect. The hymns were usually Victorian hymns, often from the children's section from the black covered Hymns Ancient and Modern Standard Edition. Inside the front cover was written the name of the Church with a warning "not to be taken away". The books were kept on a small table at the back of the Church next to the tiny stone font which stood on a stand adjacent to the table. It was in this font that I was baptised on All Souls Day - 2nd November 1940. The children took it in turns to give out the hymn books and prayer books which had minute print and were difficult to read in the rather limited light which the oil lamps gave.

Interior, Mission Church of the Good Shepherd, Hawkers Cove

You could see them better if you sat on the south side of the only aisle next to the sash window. Many of the books were old and somewhat, the worse for wear. The pages were torn and some were missing. It was frowned on if you went back to the table during the Service to find another book which had all the hymns in. It paid then to look at the hymns before the Service so that you had a book with all the hymns in and a prayer book which was intact.

The hymns and psalms were sung with great gusto and accompanied by Mrs. Frances Baker on the harmonium. It was hard work for her, pumping the little instrument, pointing the psalms, and singing at the same time, but she did that Friday evening by Friday evening and year by year. Mrs Baker lived next door to the Kinsmans at Number Five. She was a wonderful neighbour, fetching shopping from Padstow, keeping an eye on them when they were unwell. She was forthright in her conversation, vivid with her use of adjectives, usually of the kind which we were forbidden to use, but had a heart of gold. I can still hear the words of the hymns being sung by that small but enthusiastic congregation. Many of them are no longer sung. One of the favourites was 337 'There's a Friend for Little Children Above the Bright Blue Sky'. Most of the hymns contained similar sentiments but the words of these simple hymns brought to the congregation the assurance they needed; the promise of a reward for the faithful who suffered much in this life. It was comforting to know that 'there was a friend who never changes, who watched by the sick and enriched the poor' of whom I knew many in my childhood.

The Psalm was usually Psalm 23, for we knew a limited number of Psalms. We sang Psalm 46 'God is our Hope and Strength' when the weather was particularly rough. This was surely the right Psalm, with the wind blowing a Force 10 storm outside and the sound of the waves beating against the rocks nearby. The Good Shepherd, Psalm 23, reminded the congregation of coastguards, fishermen, farm labourers and their families of a Shepherd who ensured 'that they should not want.' The Psalm was sung to Hopkins in C, the set chant to the Psalm for the fourth evening of the month in the Black covered Old Cathedral Psalter.

The Old Cathedral Psalter was used at the Parish Church when I became a choirboy at the age of 10, after moving from Hawkers Cove to Padstow. The change to the Red Covered New Cathedral Psalter and, finally, to the Parish Psalter was made some years later. This was a small change but the reaction of the congregation in Padstow was vocal and unreasonable. It was as if God had been moved from his heaven. It is often the small changes in the worship of the Church which provoke the strangest outcry. The change was never made at Cove. I have a clear memory of Mrs. Baker, the organist, telling one of the Vicars, probably the Revd Ben Clarke, that if he wanted a particular hymn which she did not know he must sing it himself.

The Magnificat and Nunc Dimittis were always sung to the same chant- Smart for the former and Foster for the latter. The minor key of the Nunc Dimittis sounded like a dirge to a child, but later I came to appreciate the beauty of chants set in a minor Key. There is nothing more beautiful than a cathedral choir singing an Anglican Chant really well. Friday evening Church was a part of my life. I set out for Church about half an hour before Service time so as not to be late. This was typical of me, and, as the Church was only two minutes walk, I arrived before the Church was unlocked. My Mother came later. There was, however, a period in her life when she did not attend Church. She never forgot the failure of the then Lay Reader to visit her when my Father was killed in 1944. When she needed the comfort and support of the Church most it was not forthcoming.

I was always happy in Church in summer when they left the outside door open, but in winter it had to be closed. The closing of the door was a signal to me to flee outside into the pitch darkness of a winters night. There were no street lamps at Hawkers Cove. We always carried a torch when we walked at night from our house to that of my Grandmother. It was strange that I should fear being shut in the Church when I saw no fear in the sheer and unrelieved darkness outside. My Mother had, to her dying day, a fear of enclosed spaces and often when she went to Plymouth shopping in the large stores there she had to leave before her requirements had been purchased.

As a child I little thought that I would conduct services at Cove but in 1964-65 while I was training as a Reader I took my first Service there. It was a moving occasion for me for there were many people who had worshiped when I was a child still living in the Cove and attending Church, including Aunty Kath. She was delighted and quite excited on that occasion, but she was still not over the death of my Grandmother which had taken place some three years before.

My Grandmother's funeral was the only funeral I ever attended there. She did not die at Hawkers Cove but at the home of her youngest daughter Louvain at North Hill near Launceston. Gran had been ill for a considerable time with strokes of increasing severity and had gone with Aunty Kath to spend time at the farm there. I was in my first term of teaching at Northbourne Church of England School at Didcot, at that time. I received a telegram which told me she was very ill and a second message was brought to my lodgings by the Headteacher telling me she had died.

It was a sad journey home from Didcot to Bodmin Road on the train. I was met by Uncle Ern and my Mother at the station. We had no car at that time, indeed I could never afford a car until I became a Headteacher. It was a cold and windy late autumn evening and I was sad and tired. The journey home to Padstow of about twenty miles passed quickly, for Uncle Ern drove like Jehu in his chariot. The journey was taken up with a discussion of her last hours. She had a final massive stroke and had become deeply unconscious. She still fought for life but was worn out. Aunty Kath tried unsuccessfully to feed her. She did not want her to die for she had cared for her in a wonderful way and would soon be alone. Often, after Gran's death, she would comment on this and sadly reflect that it was wrong of her to wish her to go on living when the quality of life was gone. The struggle was too much and she died on the 23rd of October 1961. Uncle Ern had been to North Hill to see the family following her death. He had lodged with Gran and Grandad Kinsman for some time and was fond of them. Uncle Ern was a short and wiry man with a wicked sense of humour, a choice vocabulary, a happy disposition and a very kind heart. After the closure of the quarry he had looked after the machinery which remained there, for he was a self-taught but extremely gifted engineer.

It was a stormy autumn day when her funeral took place in the little Church. The Church was full, and people stood outside. The Service was conducted by the Vicar, the Revd Ben Clarke, assisted by Mr. David Griffiths, the Lay Reader. Before the Service we were placed in correct sequence, according to relationship, behind the coffin. The closest relatives were nearest to the cortege. This was always strictly observed by families. I wore my black tie and my Mother a dark coat. When my Mother's Father and Mother died there was no mourning by request so it was not worn then. On the coffin were the family wreaths. The coffin was taken into the Church through the front sash window and reverently taken out in the same way following the service. Unlike Grandad Kinsman's funeral the coffin was placed in the hearse and we followed behind in the cars. The wind was cold and gusty as we proceeded slowly along the pitted and rough road from Cove. A violent hail storm sent stinging hail stones beating on the windows of the cars and lifted a wreath off the top of the hearse. This necessitated the procession stopping and the undertaker running in an undignified manner after the wreath.

The interment in Padstow cemetery was quickly over, the strong wind carrying the words of committal away so that it was difficult to hear them. There is a finality about these words which, however much you say them or hear them, cannot fail to remind us of the fragile hold on life we all have. How often after a committal have I felt that sense of emptiness which envelops the grieving family. This is perhaps the Celtic side of my nature reacting to the gravity of the occasion.

Gran did not live to see the Church restored and repainted in 1965. The Revd David Chance, then a young student, spent some six months working in the parish prior to beginning his studies for the priesthood at Lampeter. He loved Cove and the little community and it was largely due to his youthful enthusiasm and great interest that the Church was smartened up. Electric light was installed and a new window, which he designed, of the Good Shepherd with a background of Cove and the houses was placed in the sanctuary. The family gave altar curtains in memory of Gran to the Church and my Aunts, Kathleen and Dorothy, scrubbed the Church and polished it after it had been painted by David and George Bate, two of the most faithful servants of Padstow Church. New kneelers were given to the

Church by the then Churchwarden of Padstow Church, Mr. Maurice Buckingham, as a recognition of my licensing as as Reader in March 1965.

It was always a joy to conduct a service there, for the little Church held so many memories for me. Before the service I would hurry over to see if Aunty Kath was well and coming to it. If not I would call in afterwards to see if she needed anything from Padstow.

The Church's end was tragic. One Sunday evening in April 1971 I was conducting Evensong at St. Issey Parish Church on the last Sunday of an inter-regnum there. After the service I had gone into the Vicarage to have tea with the new Incumbent, the Revd Paul Black, and his wife so it was after eight o'clock before I returned home to Padstow. On arrival my Mother greeted me with the news that our beloved Cove Church had been burnt to the ground. It was only two days before that I had been the officiant at the last service held there, the weekly Evensong. Ironically the final hymn sung was Cardinal Newman's beautiful hymn 'Lead Kindly Light'. It was sung to the Victorian tune 'Lux Benigna' written by J.B. Dykes. It was hard to believe that one of the landmarks of my childhood had disappeared. This marked the end of an era for me. How my family had loved this little Mission Church which had sustained them at the critical moments of life.

On the Monday morning I drove to Hawkers Cove. I was very unhappy and apprehensive as Cove drew ever nearer. My car passed through the last gate and began the steep descent to Hawkers Cove. There was the empty site where the Church once stood.

The only indication of its former presence was a mass of charred wood and embers with the burnt hymn books, prayer books and part of the damaged service book. I felt physically sick and deeply shocked. The little Mission Church was no more. My eyes filled with tears and I experienced that sense of emptiness and numbness that bereavement brings. Who could have done this? The official account was that there had been an electrical fault in the wiring. Various alternative rumours abounded. It is enough to say that the inhabitants of Hawkers Cove were never wholly convinced by this explanation. We will never know the truth but we all knew that something precious with so many happy memories was no more.

On my arrival at Aunty Kath's house I could see that she was visibly shaken and disturbed. By now my grandmother was dead and she lived entirely alone. The radio was silent, an air of mourning filled the house. She jumped up from the settee as I entered the room. In a voice trembling with emotion she weakly said "Our dear Church is no more, Cove will never be the same again". These words are indelibly etched on my mind. I knew how she felt for we as a family are haunted by memories and above all of the people associated with them. She mourned not only the loss of the Church, but her Father and Mother, her brother and other departed members of the family who had worshiped there. It was as if at one moment in time the losses of her life were gathered up in an intense experience of bereavement. Grief takes so many forms and this event was soul shattering.

My reaction was instant, I felt compelled to play the piano. I turned over the pages of the hymn book on the piano stand until I found the hymn 'Lead Kindly Light'. As I played the hymn from the top of the piano the whole family looked at me in solidarity, it was as if in one great chorus they were singing the words of that hymn. I felt I could even recognise their voices.

So long Thy power has blest me, sure it still,
Will lead me on,
O'er moor and fen, o'er crag and torrent, till
The night is gone.
And with the morn those Angel faces smile
Which I have loved long since, and lost awhile.

The era of Mission Churches was over and the Church was never rebuilt. Today the site serves as a parking and turning place for vehicles, but for me it will always be hallowed ground.

~ JOURNEY TO LONDON ~

Christmas was a time of magic to me, although my mother found it difficult because of its close association with my father's death. The most vivid memories of Christmas are of those I spent at Hornchurch in Essex with my Grandparents Wells and my mother in the immediate post war years. The old Carol tells of the seven joys of Mary at the birth of the Christ Child. My joys may not have numbered seven but they were many. The first joy was that of the journey by train from Padstow to Waterloo on the Atlantic Coast Express, a journey of some 260 miles taking, it seemed to me, the best part of a day. Travel was much slower after the last war than it is now.

My mother and I always spent Christmas at Hornchurch from the death of my father in 1944 until 1950 which was the last Christmas before my grandparents moved to Padstow following grandad's retirement.

We usually travelled up to London about four or five days before Christmas. My mother would be up before the crack of dawn, preparing fresh sandwiches for the train journey and making sure that nothing had been forgotten in the packing of the suitcases. When the cases were locked and she had checked that we had everything we needed she would take one of the front door keys to my aunt in the Pilot houses. While she was there Aunty Kath would wish her a happy Christmas and she would say goodbye to Gran who was still upstairs in bed. Gran was never happy about the long journey to London for it was unknown territory to her as she had never travelled further than Taunton, where one of her sisters lived. Her greatest fears occurred when I travelled from Padstow to London during the summer holidays with only the guard to keep an eye on me. It was perfectly safe in those days and I enjoyed the sense of feeling grown up. I was only seven years old when I first travelled alone to London but my grandfather was at Waterloo to meet me.

My mother was soon back. We looked out into the pitch darkness from the living room awaiting the lights of the Padstow taxi as they came into sight by Lellizzick Farm. I was always ready too soon and my excitement was such that I could not stand still. I would jump around the room asking questions about what time the taxi came and who would be driving the taxi. I was a bundle of restless energy. The train left Padstow at 8.30am and at 7.50am or there abouts Reynolds taxi would come through the gate by Lellizzick Farm and slowly descend the hill to Hawkers Cove. At the first glimpse of the headlights my mother would climb up on a chair and switch off the main switch of the electricity while I held a small torch for her to see her way down off the chair. The sound of that heavy switch marked the start of the journey proper. I rushed out into the court in front of the house carrying a small case while my mother struggled with a much larger case and locked the front door. We made our way to the top of the drive where first light was now breaking.

The taxi drove slowly up the drive and turned in the small turning area there. "May I sit in the front with Mr. Tonkin please?". My mother replied "If you are good". As the cases were being packed into the boot of the car I hopped from one leg to another as my excitement mounted. My mother climbed into the back of the taxi. She was tired but relieved that we were off to London. Her parents were a wonderful support after my Father was killed. I loved my grandparents and they were wonderful to me for, as we Cornish say, 'I was their only lamb'.

The car doors were securely shut and the car began the descent of the drive, passing the church and the boathouse. The lights of the Pilot houses shone out into the dawn of another day. We could see the front room light of Aunty Kath's house and we could make out in the half light her form at the front door. The flashing of her torch signified her presence waving us goodbye. How difficult a parting can be and we as a family are not good at saying goodbye.

Soon Cove was left far behind as the taxi slowly and laboriously made its way along the pot-holed and rutted private road for the first mile of the journey. While my mother and Mr. Tonkyn exchanged news my mind raced ahead filled with thoughts of the train journey, of my seeing my grandparents and of Christmas. After passing the gate at the end of Tregudda Lane we were on an adopted road and the car sped smoothly over the tarmaced surface and we arrived at Padstow Station in good time to catch the train.

The Atlantic Coast Express was already alongside the single platform. It consisted of the beautiful Merchant Navy Class engine and had three carriages only for the first part of the journey. We queued at the ticket office. Railway waiting rooms were a necessary evil for me. I found even the shortest wait tedious. I wanted to be in the train. The passengers in front of us bought their ticket. 'A day return to Wadebridge please'. 'A single ticket to Exeter', but we were going to London. We were now at the small window where the tickets were bought. The formidable booking clerk, Miss May Cavell, stared out through the glass partition. 'What can I do for you Mrs. Kinsmen'? 'I would like one and a half third class monthly return to London please'. The small green tickets were handed to my mother and she paid for them. As I look back to these journeys I often wonder whether my grandparents had sent the money for the fares so that we could spend Christmas with them. If not, my mother would have had to save every penny so that we could travel to London. Her savings were all spent during the years following her becoming a widow.

She wore one of the few frocks she possessed for when I was a child it was rare for her to have new clothes. I doubt if I fully realised how difficult it must have been for her in the post-war years, I was the only one who had new clothes. She skimped and saved to see that I was well dressed for she, with her great courage and determination, wanted me to have a good start in life.

May Cavell had little apparent sense of humour and when I travelled each day by train to the Grammar School I was much in awe of her stern and commanding voice. She was a lady not to be trifled with. It was Miss Cavell who had to deal with the request of Mrs. Mabel McOwen (known to us as Mrs. Ellis) when her son Willie was posted to Iceland during the war. Mrs. Ellis had decided that she would like to go there to see Willie. She imagined that Iceland was a place that could be reached by train, probably somewhere north of Plymouth. Her request for a return ticket to Iceland was met by an icy but accurate reply as Miss Cavell tartly explained that they did not issue return tickets to Iceland. Mrs. Ellis was not convinced by the reply as she felt discriminated against. Her reply was typically Cornish 'My money is as good as anyone elses'. So ended the saga of Mrs. Ellis and Miss Cavell.

It was the same Mrs. Ellis who, on hearing that whale meat was a good and probably cheaper substitute for butcher's meat, went to butcher Hawkins to ask for a whale's head for her cat.

Willie Ellis was once a member of the Parish Church Choir but singing was not his strong point so the then Vicar the Revd. Philip Slocombe, suggested that he might give his voice a rest and he became a sidesman.

Willie did not marry until after the death of his mother. His bride was a small and rather eccentric but kind hearted lady from Marazion who must have been, like him, in her mid fifties at the time of their marriage. Willie, who was incredibly mean, was known to pay his weekly grocery bill at the Co-op in pennies which were kept in a brown paper bag. The exasperated staff at the Co-op had to count these coppers, which did not endear Willie to them.

The marriage of Willie Ellis was a nine days wonder and the stories associated with it became part of the mythology of the town. Soon after his marriage he went to pay his quarterly electric bill at the South Western Electricity Board Show Rooms on the North Quay. While there he told Mr. Fred Swan, the manager, that he and his wife had not made up their minds whether to have a T.V. or a baby. It was a good job that remote control Television had not been invented.

The Atlantic Coast Express ran each day from Padstow to Waterloo and for the journey I carried with me my A.B.C. Railway Guide which my grandfather had bought me. The guide contained a map of all the railway routes in the country. My grandfather had also sent to me a list of all the stations which we would pass through on the journey, with the exact mileage of each station from Waterloo. I studied it with interest and soon knew the stations off by heart and even knew which stations were the farthest apart. The poor passengers in the carriage were given a running commentary as the train progressed along its route. My mother was slightly embarrassed with my precocious knowledge.

There was a magic about travel on a steam train which is hard to forget and the journey from Padstow to Waterloo travelled through a wide variety of scenery. The first five and a quarter miles to Wadebridge were the most beautiful. The train took nine minutes to reach Wadebridge and it was the return journey which was the best. A visitor first catching sight of the wide expanse of sand and sea from the Camel Stone Quarry must have felt, as I did, a sense of awe and wonder at the view.

I well remember my first journey home from college on a winter's day in December 1959. It was a frosty winter evening with the moon shining on the evening spring tide. The lights of Padstow twinkled out a welcome to the home-coming student. I greatly enjoyed my student days at Culham College of Education but there was something special about Padstow, for it was home. The estuary was bathed in light and shadow, and from the open carriage window in the corridor I smelt the salt air. I knew the exact points when I could first see Padstow lights, soon I would be walking along the quay and meeting fellow Padstownians and being home.

I was not so interested in the view as a young boy but was more concerned in the purpose of the journey. We had two window seats, I faced the engine so that I could see where we were going while my mother sat opposite me. The carriages then were not the open variety but each compartment was separate with a long corridor running the length of the train. There was a degree of risk in having a window seat, for when the carriage became full you had to climb over the feet and legs of fellow passengers to reach the corridor. I loved walking along the corridor and looking out of the windows.

The withered arm of the Southern Railway (formerly the London and South Western Railway) ran from Padstow to Okehampton. It was a single track with passing places at the stations. This part of the journey was remarkably slow as the track had to negotiate sharp bends and relatively steep gradients as it wended its way through the hills of Bodmin Moor and along the edge of Dartmoor.

After leaving Wadebridge the single track turned north into the heartland of North Cornwall. The train stopped at each of the little stations. Station vied with station as to which would have the finest display of flowers. The stations were beautifully maintained and on arrival the porter or ticket collector would call out proudly in Rich Cornish or Devonian accent the name of the station so as to leave the passengers in no doubt where they were. There was usually at least two or three minutes allowed for each stop. Sometimes the down train would be waiting at the opposite platform and pleasantries would be exchanged from carriage window to carriage window. The passengers who alighted from the train at these tiny stations were usually local people who had been shopping in a neighbouring town and so were known to the staff.

The 8.30am Atlantic Coast Express was the main train of the day to London. Although some local passengers used the train, most of them were bound for the larger centres of population such as Launceston, Okehampton, Exeter, Salisbury and London. Often small groups of friends would come to the station to say goodbye to the passengers. As I leant out of the window, as I did at each station, I watched as the small knot of people waving furiously grew smaller and smaller as the train gathered speed on leaving the station. It seemed at this time that the engine emitted billows of smoke and grit. You could guarantee getting a piece of grit in your eyes or a large smut on your face.

The single line track began to climb after leaving Wadebridge. The short train had not yet had additional coaches added. None were attached until Halwill Junction, where the Bude section joined the train. The Southern Railway prided itself that passengers would be able to remain in the appropriate section of the train for the whole of their journey. They could sit in the same seat then for the whole of the trip.

Beyond Camelford, Bodmin Moor came into view and the twin peaks of Brown Willy and Roughtor dominated the scene. On the back of our brown-covered exercise books at Padstow School was a map of Cornwall and beneath it was a list of Cornish rivers mountains and historical worthies. It was from here I learnt the names of these hills and their respective heights. We Cornish called them mountains while others regarded them as merely hills.

We rarely saw snow in Cornwall during my childhood. I think I must have been almost seven years of age before I saw the first heavy snowfall during that long, bitter and cruel winter of 1946-47. The intensity of the cold was added to as it was a time of great austerity for we as a country had not fully recovered from the effects of the last World War.

Brown Willy and Roughtor would, however, often be capped with snow. We could see them from the school taxi as it travelled along the high ground before descending to Padstow School. I wondered as I travelled in the train whether I might see the beauty of the silent white wilderness which heavy snowfall brings. There is a gentle and all-pervading silence following a snowstorm which seems to enfold in its grip the whole environment. It is as if we are being invited to tiptoe gently and reverently upon the virgin snow. Often it is only the small claw marks of the birds which dent the top of the pure, unspotted, freshly-fallen snow.

A more familiar view was of a landscape sodden from prolonged winter rain, with pools of brown muddy water lying at regular intervals on the rough upland pasture. Small muddy trails made by the sheep and cattle became almost impassable in winter as this was the wettest part of Cornwall with almost double the rainfall of the coastal belt. If a gale was blowing you would see groups of cattle huddling together under the stone hedgerow seeking shelter on the lew side of the hedge from the prevailing South Westerly Atlantic winds. The trees had been trained by the majesty of the winds to bow before them

Padstow Station

and point away from the intensity of their blast. On other occasions the whole damp region would be blanketed by mist so that you could barely see the fence at the side of the track from the train window. No two journeys were ever the same. This was the excitement and adventure of travel to me as a child. The constantly changing weather which we experience is one of the joys of living in a battle zone between Atlantic and Continental Airstreams.

Before we reached Launceston it would be time to have a drink. My mother would either have a cup of tea, or sometimes coffee, from her thermos flask while I drank orange juice or lemon juice. I rarely drank tea or coffee as a child. There would also be a biscuit or a bun. Clear instructions were issued by my mother 'You must sit still while you drink your drink, otherwise it will be spilt'. She had visions of my baptising other people in the compartment with sticky orange juice.

On one well remembered occasion in my childhood my mother poured a cup of water over my head. I was being especially aggravating on this occasion. It was a particularly hot summer day and I was wearing only my swimming costume. I had been playing in the courtyard outside our house. The intense heat of the day had made me thirsty. I opened the door and called "Mum, May I have a cup of orange juice, please ?" She promptly gave me a drink of this. By then I had quickly changed my mind. 'I would rather have a glass of water'. This request was acceded to less rapidly. I was still not satisfied and decided that I would perhaps prefer the orange after all. By now my very busy mother was distinctly annoyed and I received a dowsing from the cup of water which was in her hand. After this I was always careful to ask for what I really wanted to drink.

Launceston Southern Station was situated at the bottom of the valley between the town of Launceston and St. Stephens, Launceston on the opposite hill side. It was the last station before we left Cornwall to go into England. It was a busy station, particularly on market days. Stations always seemed to be a hub of activity to a small child. You could look up the hill to where Launceston castle stood sentinel over this former capital of Cornwall or you could view the opposite hill, where the original settlement had been, and see St. Stephen's Launceston tall tower. By now I was becoming rather restless for the journey seemed interminable. Patience is a virtue that only began to develop as I grew older.

We left Launceston and crossed the bridge over the River Tamar into Devon. The other passengers in the compartment smiled sweetly at me although I suspect they were tired of the incessant chatter of this highly-strung and excitable child who had a fount of information which may have enthralled him but seemed to others a sign of precocity! The Tamar nearly makes Launceston into an island. 'If it were three miles longer we would live on an island' I proudly informed the other passengers. My mother glared at me, making faces which meant "be quiet and give other people some peace". She always told her friends that I was vaccinated with a gramophone needle.

As the train trundled over the railway bridge into Devon we waved Cornwall au revoir. After my father was killed my grandparents Wells wanted my mother to go back to London to live. In many ways this made sense, for there she could command a much better income with her commercial training and skills. She did not want to leave Cornwall as she had become deeply attached to it and had made many friends. Her major reason, I learnt as I grew up, was that she considered Cornwall to be a far better environment for me. I am eternally grateful to her that I was privileged to have my childhood in the beautiful surroundings of Cove and Padstow.

Halwill Junction was the scene of the first additional coaches being added to the train. The two carriages from Bude were already standing alongside the platform from where the Bude branch left. They never seemed to be particularly crowded.

The train stopped there until the Bude section was coupled up to the main train. You felt the impact as the buffers of the new section connected with our part of the express. After about ten minutes we were off again. The train wended its way like a gigantic snake through the upland surrounding Dartmoor. The last of the stations on the withered arm was the tiny halt of Maddaford Moor. It seemed to be miles away from anywhere, but there were usually one or two passengers alighting or boarding the train. We joined the Plymouth line at Meldon Junction and from there onwards the track was a double one. Okehampton meant the addition of the Plymouth coaches and the restaurant car. (In summer this was part of the train all the way from Padstow).

The pace of the journey quickened after leaving Okehampton and we were soon at Exeter. I was always puzzled by the approach to St. David's station. The Southern Railway joined the main Paddington-Penzance Great Western line at Cowley Bridge. We then proceeded to St. David's Station. The main Great Western Route was running alongside the Southern track. The down trains of the Great Western Railway ran parallel with the up train of the Southern Railway. Although I had a good sense of direction I found this difficult to understand. After a brief stop at St. David's the train climbed the steep incline to Exeter Central passing through a tunnel on the way. Exeter Central station was overlooked by Exeter Prison and, as the train stopped there for several minutes, it was possible to have a walk along the platform. I imagined that the prisoners were looking out from the cells at the railway station, perhaps secretly hoping to escape and join the passengers on the train. One of the familiar figures of my childhood journeys was a black dog, probably a labrador, who boarded the train with its owner collecting for the blind. I was allowed to put coppers into the tin which was attached to its back. I had often wondered and feared what it would be like to be blind. On occasions I had shut my eyes and tried to walk on the sand on the beach. The darkness of the blind person's world did not appeal to me. My mother had explained how guide dogs for the blind helped them to move around, but it was so difficult for me as a child to comprehend this. My reaction was one of intense sorrow and unhappiness that people could not see. The emotions of childhood form the basis of the empathy which mature adults are able to give to those who are handicapped in life. I have never found it a problem to feel what it is like to stand in another's shoes.

The last part of the journey from Exeter to London passed more quickly. The train gathered speed and it was almost impossible to read the mileage on the mile posts by the side of the track. I liked to read them and say we are only so many miles from London. The train stopped at a few more stations en route and we were soon approaching London. About half an hour before arrival at Waterloo my excitement level reached fever pitch. My heart thumped with anticipation at the thought of seeing my grandparents. I would have so much to tell them of the journey and its events. The views from the window changed as we approached London. By the time we were in suburbia the rows and rows of houses had begun to put their evening lights on. There is a great fascination about a lighted window when the curtains are not drawn. It is as if you are sharing, even remotely, in the life of the family there. Small semi-detached suburban houses could be seen from the train and in many of them you could see preparation being made for afternoon tea or for the evening meal. It was almost dark by now.

When we were within about ten minutes of our destination I was sent to the toilet with strict instructions to wash my grubby hands. Trains always seemed to be rather shabby in immediate post-war days. The toilet on the train was not like our flush lavatory at the Coastguard Station. You pressed a raised button on the floor and the contents from it disappeared onto the track below. The roller towel was by now fully used up and there was rarely any soap or toilet paper at the end of the journey. The hot water was usually cold and often only dribbled from the tap. I dipped my hand into the tepid water which barely covered the bottom of the bowl and wiped the dirt on to the towel. I combed my untidy hair with the comb I had been given by my mother for this purpose and returned to the carriage.

The train began to slow down, the cases were lifted down from the rack above. At regular intervals I was told to sit still as we should soon be in London. The very name conjured up for me the visits I would make to the Tower of London, Madame Tassauds, and the Zoo. The warm and comfortable small bungalow at Hornchurch was a source of happiness to me.

Waterloo Station with its twenty platforms seemed so gigantic and noisy. As the train pulled into the platform you hoped that the platform might be on the same side as the window seats we occupied. It usually was. "Don't open the door until the train has stopped, and wait for me to get out first", my mother firmly said. If I had had my way I would have been running along the platform to find if Grandad was there. We said goodbye to our fellow passengers and walked briskly along the crowded platform.

At last, through the milling crowds, we saw Grandad Wells. He was looking out for us and eventually he spotted my mother and me. His first action was to take the heaviest of the cases from her and to inquire what kind of journey we had had. I was anxious to talk to him about all that I had seen and especially about the stations which I had learnt from his list.

Grandad Wells was a tall man, about six feet in height. He was one of Pharaoh's 'lean kine' with little or no spare flesh on his sparse frame. His sight was not too good and he had begun to develop cataracts in his eyes about the time of retirement. He worked at the office of Samuel Hansons and Sons in Eastcheap from the time he left school at the age of fourteen until his retirement on his sixty-fifth birthday. He was a very hard-working and capable office worker and was held in high esteem by the firm and by his fellow workers.

The office in which he worked was below ground level so he worked the whole of the time in artificial light. I remember visiting his office and seeing his fellow employees who I had known, from his conversation, as real people.

Grandad Wells was the tenth of the eleven children of Henry and Annie Eleanor Wells (nee Smith). All of them were boys except for Ethel who died, I believe of scarlet fever, while still a small child, and Annie who died of T.B. The Wells family were intelligent and gifted but with very quick and fiery tempers. I knew none of his brothers but had heard much of them while listening to the family discussing events which belonged to the history of the Wells family. One of his brothers was the champion cornet player of England, and music played a significant part in their lives. Grandad played the organ when younger and had a fine baritone voice and a deep love of music. He encouraged my mother to learn to play the piano and also the violin. Grandad would play the organ while my mother accompanied him on the piano. Gran Wells would listen appreciatively but could not even sing in tune, although her eldest sister, Annie, had a fine singing voice. I loved music from my earliest childhood and today it provides me with a great source of consolation when I am depressed. I can work out my sadness by playing the piano. Music has the power to stir my highly emotional nature and stimulate within me the urge to write.

It was from Grandad Wells that I have inherited my deep and enduring love of history. His active, intelligent and perceptive mind was coupled with a remarkable memory. My mother was very like her father in ways and, although I am very much a Kinsman in looks and in temperament, I am fortunate that they have passed on to me the power to recall incidents and events with clarity. I would like to think that I have their perception and ability to assess people and situations accurately. Grandad had the gift of making history live. We would discuss the names and dates of the Kings and Queens of

Winnie & Barry Kinsmen

England for hours. This was the type of history he learnt at the Elementary School at West Ham in his childhood. He had the remarkable feat of having a medal for full attendance for the whole of each school year with the exception of one. Indeed in his school days children were placed in position in class according to their weekly performance in tests at the end of each week. He occupied the first position for all but one week.

By the time I was eight I was able to recite in correct sequence, with dates of accession and death or abdication, all the rulers of England from Egbert, King of Wessex, who was probably the first King who claimed anything approaching a national influence as ruler. I was proud of this knowledge but I am certain that my friends regarded my recital of this string of names and dates as boring and totally irrelevant to their immediate interests.

After leaving the platform at Waterloo we descended by moving staircase or, more correctly, escalator to the underground. I was never very happy about stepping on or off it but I loved the descent to the bowels of the earth and the rush of warm air and the particular smell associated with the tube. This was a totally different but equally fascinating world from my Cornish childhood. The density of travellers, many of whom carried brief cases with rolled umbrellas resting on their arms and dressed in pin stripe trousers and wearing bowler hats, amazed me. Bowler hats were worn only at funerals in Cornwall. I missed, however, the cheery smiles and the friendly greetings which were so much part of Cornish life. These travellers rarely smiled, or so it appeared to me.

The approach of the tube train emerging noisily from the dark subterranean hole and the hiss of the brakes as the train rattled to a standstill would give way to the mad scramble to enter the train while the doors were open. How I feared being jammed in the doors or taken on to the next station while Grandad and my mother were boarding the train. We changed at Charing Cross on to the District line which took us all the way to Hornchurch Station.

My grandfather recalled as we travelled, at first underground and then, as we began to leave the central part of London behind, above ground, what it was like when he first travelled to work at the turn of the century. The first underground trains were steam and the tunnels soon became filled with the black sulphurous emission from the engine pulling the train. He also described the surprise which those travelling above ground must have had when the smoke emerged periodically from the vents which allowed smoke to escape from the dark tunnels below.

To a young and imaginative child, the rows and rows of terraced houses and semi-detached houses and bungalows which lined the side of the track for the whole of the journey were so different from the scattered settlements which I had grown up with in Cornwall. Grandad had been born in West Ham (now Newham) and had moved gradually further out of London as London had expanded in the years between the wars. He had witnessed the disappearance of farm land under the massive brick intrusion which preceded the more controlled planning of post war years.

The underground trains were very crowded, as we arrived at Waterloo at the beginning of the rush hours. I had not learnt the art of balancing while the train lollopped and swayed its way along the electrified rails which were pointed out to me as a potential killers if you were unfortunate enough to fall on the live rail. The commuters took the noisy and exhausting journey for granted. My grandfather knew that when he returned from work Gran Wells would have a nourishing and hot meal ready for him and that, when the evenings were light, he could relax in his beautiful garden which was his pride and joy. The underground network was displayed on the inside of each carriage and the names of the various lines with their stations were already known to me. There is a tremendous power in a name, particularly ones which have a real association with events happy and sad which we experienced in the formative years of our lives. My particular favourites were Tower Hill, where we alighted when we visited the Tower of London, Monument, which was near to the spot where the great Fire of London started, Regents Park, which conjured up the wide variety of animals which I saw on visits to London Zoo, and South Kensington, for there I could spend hours exploring the Science and Natural History museums. On this occasion however, each stop meant that there were only five, four, three, two and finally one station before we reached Hornchurch, which was our destination. There was still a walk of about half a mile to go before we reached the Wells bungalow but, as we were tired, it was usually in a taxi that the long and exciting journey was completed.

The taxi sped along Kenilworth Gardens with its large semi-detached bungalows and houses and the tree-lined pavements which were so much part of the suburbs built between the wars. It was along this pavement that I would walk on the frequent trips I made with my grandparents to the shops or to the station. When I had a tricycle for Christmas when I was about eight years of age, I rode along the pavement with such pride and determination that I could have been the successful winner of the twenty-four hour race at Le Mans.

I was usually careful to avoid walking on any cracks in the pavement, for in my rich imaginary world this spelt danger. As I cycled along at weekends there would be the smell of a bonfire in one of the nearby gardens. It seemed that everyone in those days spent their weekends in their neatly tended gardens. If I spent my Easter holidays at Hornchurch the cherry and apple blossom was at its best and the pavement would be carpeted with the pink blossoms which had gently dropped from the heavy laden branches above. The trees seemed so still for at home in Cornwall there were few of these and they were usually in constant motion dancing to the tunes of the Atlantic gales.

The taxi turned to the right into Belmont Road where the second bungalow on the right was Tregudda, my grandparents home. "Have you been to India?" a neighbour inquired of my grandfather soon after they moved into Belmont Road in 1934. 'No' he replied. "But I have been to Cornwall". The Wells loved Cornwall and it became their greatest joy to spend a fortnights holiday each year at Cove. After my mother had settled there, particularly during the war years, Gran spent a great deal of her time with us.

Tregudda was named after the gorge which was about a mile from Cove. It was his favourite spot and he loved to walk the coastal path from Tregudda Gorge to Cove. The gentle springy turf, the myriads of sea pinks and the restless Atlantic haunted him until his dying day. Tregudda was a favourite place for picnics when I was a child. There was a real sun trap there where you could find shelter from the wind on most occasions, a rare spot in the windswept landscape. Cornish gales are lazy winds, they blow right through you.

Tregudda was a small semi-detached bungalow, built in the early 1930's, with a small front garden but a much larger one at the rear. The lights were already on as we drew up outside the front gate, which was set into a low wooden fence which Grandfather Wells periodically creosoted. He paid for the taxi while I bounded out on to the pavement. I knew that Gran Wells would have probably seen the arrival of the taxi and, sure enough, the front door was opened and she stood waiting to welcome us. She had the most beautiful long auburn hair which never turned grey even though she lived to be 86. The hair was plaited on top of her head and each morning she combed her waist length hair which hung mermaid like down her back. Her rosy cheeks and twinkling eyes beamed out the warmest of welcomes.

May Wells (nee Clare) was the fifth child and youngest of the three daughters of William and Hannah Clare. She had a younger brother, Tom, who she always referred to as 'Jubilee Baby Clare' as he was born in 1887, the year of Queen Victoria's Golden Jubilee. She was one of the most placid people I have ever known. Her disposition could only best be described as sunny. She beamed her way through life. She was totally devoted to her husband Jim. Jim made all the decisions while she dutifully maintained a happy home, cooking, mending, and cleaning the bungalow. She never had to make a difficult decision in her long life. Grandad Wells did all the thinking for her, and when he died my mother took over. She was totally fulfiled in her role as a housewife and would never have understood any form of feminism. I suspect my grandfather told her how to vote at the time of any elections. He was devoted to her however, and when they walked out together, it was always arm in arm. If ever there was a happy marriage, this was it.

Once safely in the bungalow, the events of the journey were unfolded to her by me at lightning speed. She simply smiled and listened, for she was an excellent listener. My mother was exhausted after the long journey and my grandfather was ready to smoke his sweet-smelling tobacco. 'We will unpack after you have had your meal'. 'Why don't you all go and sit down while I finish serving out the meal?' Grandad decided that she needed help so he went into the small kitchen (Probably best described as a kitchenette).

Gran Wells cooked by gas, which was unknown to me at that time. In this kitchen there was a small Ideal boiler which heated the hot water as well as giving warmth to the room. The Ideal boiler was kept burning all the time in winter but had to be periodically cleared out and re-lit. Gran used a gas poker to do this. The Wells were great believers in the use of gas as Grandad Wells father worked for the Gas, Light and Coke Company at Stratford for much of his working life as did some of his brothers. One was a Solicitor for the firm. The bungalow was, however lit with electricity but the street lights in Belmont Road were still gas. There was a deep mellowness and friendliness about the gas lamp outside the bungalow which shone its cheery beams into the small front bedroom where I slept. This was particularly cheering when I was alone in the small bedroom.

The Christmas decorations were never put up before Christmas Eve and so the bungalow was not yet decorated for the great festival. The chains and Christmas Tree decorations, which were used year after year, were kept in old shoe boxes neatly labelled 'Christmas Decorations' in the sideboard in the dining room.

We sat down to a delicious evening meal, which was usually Roast Beef with greens, peas and parsnips. Grandad Wells loved beef, so each Sunday when the customary roast dinner was eaten it had to be beef with Yorkshire Pudding. Gran had prepared horse-radish sauce to give added flavour to the beef, she made her own from fresh horse-radishes bought from Romford Market. My first experience of eating this horse-radish sauce was here. However, it was very hot and I unwisely took too much. I coughed, spluttered, and nearly choked as it burnt my mouth, causing my eyes to water. 'You won't take so much again' my mother observed, while Gran kindly suggested that I might like a drink of water. Gran spoilt her only grandchild while Grandad did not. His support and love were of a disciplined kind. I was wary of transgressing the perimeters of acceptable behaviour which he firmly maintained.

After the meal I was allowed to stay up a little later than I did at home. There were definite routines observed here. The six o'clock news and the nine o'clock news formed the centre of the ritual. I had to be quiet while the news was being broadcast. This was a great hardship, as there were always questions I wanted to ask about news items. After the news Grandad would read either the News Chronicle, which was his daily paper, or the Evening Standard, which he had bought at Fenchurch Street Station before his evening journey home. He read this fine paper until his death, and would have greatly mourned its passing. He regarded it as a suitable one to have in his home while my mother was a child.

I was never quite certain of his political views as he was very much his own man. He was basically liberal in outlook and I rather suspect voted Liberal on a number or most occasions in his life. He was an Asquithian Liberal and had a strong dislike of Lloyd George, for he believed Lloyd George had helped to destroy the Liberal Party. His dislike of Lloyd George was only exceeded by his views of the Post-War Labour Government. His most acerbic comments were reserved for Sir Stafford Cripps and Edith Summerskill. Gran Wells had come from a Liberal family and her father had been an active canvasser for Sir John Simon. In her later years she voted for John Pardoe, who was a greatly respected Liberal M.P. for North Cornwall.

You knew exactly where you stood with Grandad Wells. He was as straight as a die and yet his firm views and strict appearance belied an inner kindness and generosity. He would help anyone in trouble. While Grandad read the paper or listened to the wireless Gran would do her mending or crocheting. She was very skilled at this. One of the most surprising gifts which Grandad Wells possessed was the ability to knit with great speed. He knitted christening robes for families and friends. He knitted all the gloves and mittens for his wife and daughter and even my socks. This was therapeutic. Grandad Wells needed to relax as he was a great worrier and lived life to a great intensity. He had a history of stomach problems which were probably largely due to his over-conscientious nature.

Bedtime in the bungalow at Hornchurch was so different from Cove. The bungalow was small and compact so I could lie in bed and hear the conversation coming from the dining room where Gran, Grandad and my mother talked, or I could hear the cheery tones of the light classical music which was the type of music they particularly enjoyed. On Sunday evenings to listen to Grand Hotel and Albert Sadler and the Palm Court Orchestra followed by Sunday Half Hour. Hymns were a great favourite with his generation although while living at Hornchurch they did not attend church. It was only at Padstow that they resumed regular attendance at a place of worship.

The front bedroom of the bungalow was a very small room and the iron double-bedstead stood against the wall so that to climb into the inner side of the bed meant clambering across the bed. The bed had an old feather tye underneath and it was remarkably comfortable. The gas lamp on the pavement outside shone its mellow light right into the bedroom and cast its shadow across the bed. I loved lying in the bed listening to the conversation of the family or the music of the wireless playing within earshot. There was a deep security associated with this bungalow. Sleep came so easily in these surroundings.

I did not sleep particularly well as a child but at Hornchurch I slept better than at home at Cove. I was tired after the long journey to London and the thoughts of the next day filled my mind as I drifted gently into a deep contented sleep.

I was always awake very early, long before it was daylight, but already Grandad Wells was up. He was off to work soon after seven and before he set off we were all given a cup of tea in bed. The sounds of the clatter of cups in the kitchen and the whistle from the whistling kettle were coupled with the wireless quietly announcing the early morning news. Grandad always cleaned the grate in the dining room before setting off to work. When he had left I ran into Gran and Grandad's back bedroom and jumped into bed alongside Gran, for I knew that she would tell me the stories and recite me the poems or recitations she knew so well. She had a tiny hand puppet, a monkey named Susan, which I was allowed to put on my hand after she had talked to me in a monkey voice which purported to be that of the greatly-loved Susan. Susan must have belonged to my mother as a small girl and even pre-dated her childhood. I had numerous conversations with her while Gran would answer her part. Gran had a good sense of humour and eyes that twinkled when she told a story or recounted the many events of her childhood. Her father was a builder, her mother somewhat of a hypochondriac who she admitted did very little in the house except produce the children. Great-grandad Clare even cooked the meals. She loved her father and was a little critical of her mother. Mild criticism was the strongest of her negative emotions. My mother did not care much for her maternal grandmother and even less for her spinster sister, Amy, who was a typical schoolmarm. My mother never conformed to the ideas which they had of a child. She was in many ways a rebel with the Wells' individualistic streak strongly to the fore.

There was a tremendous bond between Gran Wells and myself. I suppose she had time to talk and tell the stories which I loved. She was warm, with a natural radiance which her marvellous disposition exuded. She was in tune with the world and so contented with her life and the perfect foil for Grandad, who needed his placid and good-natured wife. She questioned nothing, she accepted life, she believed in people and in God. Her faith was simple, easy and natural. When she died I chose the hymn of John Greenleaf Whittier 'Dear Lord and Father of Mankind' which contains the line 'In simple trust like those who heard beside the Syria Sea, the gracious calling of the Lord' for her funeral. She loved people and was always considered a wonderful neighbour.

There were a few things which she did not approve of and one of them was 'housing'. Although she was loved by her neighbours she never ventured into their homes while Grandad was at work. Her life was fulfiled within the boundaries of her home. She was well organised and each day had a set routine which ensured that the beds were made, the house cleaned, good meals regularly cooked and, above all, it was a real home for Grandad. Her whole life revolved around him and she waited happily for his return from the office each day.

Christmas Eve was a great day for me, for the decorations were put up and the Christmas Tree adorned. The tree had been bought by Grandad in London and came home with him on the day before Christmas Eve. It was to stand in the bay window in a large tub filled with earth from the garden. The tub was enclosed in crepe paper. The little decorations and paper chains were placed on the thin needle-laden branches. The tree smelt beautiful with its pervading smell of pine. On the top of the tree a small fairy was placed. The tree would stand there until Twelfth Night and each day the fallen needles would be swept up. The tree had no lights on or even silver balls yet it had, to a child, a magical quality.

The bay-windows, as well as having curtains which we drew at night, had a thinner green over-curtain which ran on a runner and was drawn after the curtains had been closed. This was to help to keep out the cold, but at Christmas a large silver star was pinned in the middle of it.

Four paper chains were placed diagonally from corner to corner of the dining room and above the mantelpiece two round paper chain balls were hung. This was the measure of the decorations for it would be wrong to over-decorate the room. In the centre of the ceiling hung the round bowl containing the electric light with a 150 watt bulb inside.

On the sideboard was placed a glass bowl with apples and oranges in and, after their post-war reappearance, bananas. There were also some tangerines when available. In another bowl were the nuts, brazil nuts, walnuts, almonds and hazel nuts. Next to the bowl were the nutcrackers. On the green runner on top of the sideboard was a packet of sticky dates with a small wooden pick to lift them from the oblong

Tregudda Gorge

box with rounded corners. Grandad would split open a date and place a brazil nut in it. This was delicious. Sometimes there were chestnuts which would be roasted on the coal fire in the evenings. If the fire was right, toast would be toasted on the adjustable fork. I have never since tasted toast like this. Sometimes sugar would be sprinkled on it and, of course, butter. The toasting fork intrigued me and when the family were not in sight I would charge around the room using it as a weapon of war.

A bottle of port was purchased for Christmas but this was kept inside the sideboard and only taken out after the Christmas Dinner when Grandad drunk a glass of it. Gran would have half a glass as she said "port went to her head or even to her legs". Her rosy cheeks seemed scarlet after this tiny tipple. My mother had her glass and I was allowed some in a glass too. My mother maintained that by allowing me a little drink on special occasions at home I would never become a heavy drinker. This was yet another example of her clever parenting. I never remember sherry being drunk during my childhood.

On Christmas Eve I was put to bed early so as to be asleep when Father Christmas came. A stocking was tied to the head of the bed and a pillow-case left beside the bed. It was carefully explained to me that Father Christmas would come through the door, which was left unlocked so that he could enter. They guessed that I would find it hard to believe he would come down the chimney as there was not enough space for him to do so. There was only one chimney in the bungalow which was in the dining

Jim & May Wells (maternal grandparents)

room, and that was far too small for him.

How hard it was to sleep that night. My mother shared the bed with me as there were only two bedrooms in the bungalow. I kept on waking up and asking whether he had been and was told to go to sleep. I wonder what thoughts went through her mind during the long hours of that night for her. She was probably remembering Christmases when dad was alive and, above all, that fateful Christmas of 1944. The anniversary of a loved one's death is always a time of difficulty but as she heard on Christmas Eve the happiest time of the year became the time when his absence was most noted.

The last Christmas of my mother's life was perhaps the most difficult. She was obviously very unwell and losing weight quite rapidly. Her appetite was disappearing. I sensed that she was not well. Her last appearance at St. Issey Church was for the children's Carol Service on the Sunday before Christmas and when I returned from celebrating the Midnight Mass she was in bed. Usually she waited up for my return, after she stopped attending herself, to hear all about it.

She cooked the Christmas Dinner with all its trimmings but ate little herself. This was an act of great courage as she must have known that this was to be her last Christmas. We had a duck that year and it was served with orange sauce and stuffing. The cauliflower had its own white sauce. The roast potatoes and peas filled my plate. There was the usual Christmas pudding and rum sauce. It was a beautiful meal.. While I enjoyed this she was being eaten up by terminal cancer which was not discovered until a post mortem was conducted following her death. It was so hard to convince the hospital staff during her last illness that she was dying. Hospitals cannot always deal with death and so make it much harder for those relations who know what is happening. The fact that I was told each time I stated that she was terminally ill that they had no evidence of this made it so much harder. She knew, I knew, but they did not.

At about five in the morning the bedroom light was finally switched on, my mother having realised that sleep was impossible for either of us. She took the stocking off the iron bedpost and gave it to me. The stocking usually contained an apple, an orange, some nuts and also a small book. When I was very small there were Mary Mouse books in my stocking. The major present was either in the pillow-case or by the side of the bed. On successive Christmases there was a cricket bat, a tricycle and a wind-up gramophone. The cricket bat was one of my prized childhood possessions as I loved cricket and the gramophone, too, was one of the joys of my childhood as I love music.

Well before six I was running into my grandparents' bedroom to show them my presents. Christmas was easier for them and there was a natural happiness in the pleasure of seeing my great pleasure in receiving those lovely presents.

Grandad Wells was always the first one up, even on Christmas Morning, and the whole family were in circulation by seven o'clock. His generation did not lie in bed late even when they had the opportunity to do so.

The little kitchen was soon full of various saucepan's which would later be filled with vegetables to accompany the Christmas Roast. The chicken or goose had been stuffed the day before. I can see my grandmother's needle poised as delicately as a surgeon's scalpel sewing up part of the bird at the end of the operation. The stuffing was usually thyme stuffing as Grandad Wells did not like sage and onion stuffing. His likes and dislikes prevailed.

The little kitchen soon became very hot as the bird was placed in very early and cooked slowly so that it would be really tender. The oven of the gas stove and the gas rings on the top worked overtime that day. Later in the morning the window would be open and the back door left ajar to let out the steam from the saucepan's as they bubbled and boiled.

After a light breakfast I was taken for a long walk by Grandad while the ladies prepared the dinner. Grandad Wells was a prodigious walker and I loved the long walks which he took me on. These were times when his great skill in remembering events of his childhood were of great interest to me. One of the most graphic of all of his memories was that of the funeral of Queen Victoria in January 1901. He remembered the horses, with their black plumes, as they pulled the cortege through the streets of London. The end of the longest reign in English History was indelibly etched on his mind. He was sixteen at the time. This led on to the Coronation of King Edward VII which had to be postponed as the King elect had had his appendix removed near to the time originally fixed for his Coronation.

The lives of the Royal Family and their relationship to other European Royal Families were also part of the knowledge he imparted to me. In his bookcase was an old and valued Whittaker's Almanac which he would take out and show me. This compendium of information was one of my favourite books in my later childhood. He gave me one on my eleventh birthday. We spent hours looking together at various sections of the book which acted as a stimulus for his incredible memory.

The walks in Hornchurch were so different from those of my Cornish childhood. We mostly walked along the side streets of the town but occasionally we walked far enough to reach the countryside around the built-up area. It was so flat after the hilly terrain of Padstow. When I had a tricycle the pavements were ideal for cycling on. We knew all the streets for miles around.

There was a fine park in Hornchurch which provided a contrast to the densely built up town. It was in this park that we went to watch cricket when I spent my summer holidays with my grandparents. There was a serenity about Saturday afternoon cricket matches then. The only sounds were those of bat striking ball. The subtle variations of sound reflected the nature of the stroke played. The best sound was that of a perfectly executed stroke with ball firmly played with the middle of the bat. The sound of a snick to slip or gully was less satisfying. You could shut your eyes and gauge how well a batsman was playing simply by listening to the sound of bat on ball or to the raucous cries of fielder appealing for leg-before-wicket or a catch. The cries varied in intensity, some were routine cries which contained little but hope while others were of a intent when certainty of appeal was the order of the day. The ripple of applause as the ball raced across the boundary seemed so very right to me then. The noise of the cricket crowds today reflects the changed nature of the game. One day matches were unheard of at county and country level. Grandad Wells had a great knowledge of the game and would discuss the great heroes of his young days. His particular county Essex, had at that time never won a county championship but he followed them with interest and loyal support One of the great batsman he recalled with affection was Perrin. He described him as a lazy batsman, for most of his runs came in boundaries, the implication being that he did not run the opportune singles.

One of the greatest thrills of my childhood was the visit to Southchurch Park at Southend to see the West Indies play Essex in the summer of 1950. Those great spin bowlers of calypso fame Ramadin and Valentine had wrecked havoc with the English batsman during that summer. We sat in our deckchairs watching Sonny Ramadin bowl. One of the men sitting near to us allowed us use of his binoculars with which he tried to spot the 'wrong un' which he bowled. The guile of great spin bowling has sadly beep replaced by the brute force of fast bowling. A contest between a spinner and batsman was one not only of skill but of intelligence. One of my grandad's favourite expressions of a good slow bowler was that he bowled 'with his head'. It was only as I grew older that I realised the true significance of his remarks.

I had to learn to score and had been given a little score book as a present. Charlie Harvey, who taught at Padstow school for many years and was a great fan of cricket, taught me how to score. We were allowed, at dinner time, to go into his classroom and listen to the commentary on radio from the various test match grounds. Scoring appealed to me and I would sit at home on Saturday listening to the commentaries and scoring with meticulous care in my little score book. When I was a little older I took my score book to the Padstow Ground at Three Turning and was allowed to help with the scoring putting up the metal number plates on the scoreboard.

We were always back in good time for the Christmas Dinner. The table was by now laid with the special Christmas table cloth on it. Sounds of the meal being dished up came from the little kitchen and, soon after midday, the hot plates were brought in and the delicious meal began. We had Christmas crackers by our plates and the room was filled with a sense of well-being.

When I was about eight I won a goose in a raffle organised by Mr. Johnny Warden who was one of the hairdressers at Padstow. I sat for hours in the little barber shop waiting for my hair to be cut. The shop was filled with conversation and smoke and the news of the town frequently exchanged. Ivy Warden, his wife, sat on a form and knitted vigorously while her husband cut the hair. There was a 'little tiny' shop at the front of the building and periodically she would disappear into the shop to serve a customer with cigarettes or other items. When my turn came to have my hair cut I would sit on a small board placed across the round chair with arms. Johnny would chat incessantly and would amuse us children with little tricks like producing cigarettes from his ears. He was a jovial man, much involved in the life of the town especially with the Blue Ribbon Oss and later with the Padstow Carollers. It fascinated me to watch him shave some of the older men with his cut-throat razor and to see their faces covered with huge suds of lather. He also singed the ends of peoples' hair, and then the small room was filled with a very unpleasant aroma. He worked long hours and there always seemed to be a room full of people.

The goose, which I was convinced I would win, made a marvellous Christmas Dinner. I had said for weeks that I would win it while my mother said that only one of those who entered the raffle could possibly win. This did not shake my confidence in any way. I never did anything without being convinced of the outcome although I was very tentative in new situations.

The Christmas dinner with the bird, roast potatoes, peas, carrots, and usually cauliflower and brussels filled the plate. My mother knew that I was a faddy child and before I began to eat it I was told to 'eat what you can but do not make comments on why you are leaving a particular part of the meal'. I usually managed to eat most of the meal which was followed by Christmas pudding and custard, often with brandy in it. The Christmas Pudding always contained silver threepenny bits which I could keep and add to my coin collection. Gran always managed to serve me a slice with a coin in. She was determined I should have one.

We sat at table for a longer time than usual on Christmas Day. Family meals are to be enjoyed and conversation is an essential part of the occasion. Dear, wise Grandad had a very positive outlook and was a shrewd judge of people and situations. He had a few prejudices, which was to be expected from his Victorian lower middle class background. He had a definite dislike of 'High Church' and would often tell me about churches where there was advanced ceremonial and doctrines usually associated with Roman Catholicism! 'If they want this they should become Roman Catholics' he would often say. He had been brought up in a Free Church background but had attended West Ham Parish Church in his younger days. This church was decidedly 'Low Church' and preaching was considered to be the main element of worship. He talked of the great preachers of the early years of the century and the inter-war years. He considered Maude Royden to be one of these. I learned of Dean Inge, Woodbine Willie and Dick Sheppard from him. He disliked Donald Soper for his pacifist views and would drive home his arguments against pacifism by recalling what Donald Soper told a questioner who asked him 'What would you do to stop a man who was trying to rape your daughter' 'Reason with him'. Those words were spoken with a deep degree of disdain. Grandad, who was not a violent man, would say 'I know what I would do'.

Another of his deep dislikes was the then M.P. for Hornchurch, Geoffrey Byng. He never liked the Post War Labour Government but was not a supporter of the Tory position. He had a basic liberalism about his attitude.

After the meal was cleared away and the dishes and pots and pans washed up we all sat listening to the radio, especially to the King's speech. This was the highlight of the programmes on Christmas Day and I was expected to listen to this in complete silence. My mother watched me intently to see that this rule was maintained.

As the shades of the winter late afternoon grew, the fire lit up the room casting shadows on the furniture. The mellow gas-light outside in the street entered the room. The curtains were always drawn before the electric light was switched on. There was only a central light enclosed within a glass bowl which gave an even light to the room. Sometimes on Christmas afternoon the adults dozed contentedly and the room became almost dark before the light was put on. I was content listening to the radio or even looking out of the window into the front garden and street beyond. I was secure within this happy environment with their love surrounding me. Soon after four o'clock tea was served. It was a light tea with bread and butter and homemade jam, usually plum for that was Grandad's favourite. There were little iced cakes with jam in and, of course, a Christmas cake and usually a cake with chocolate icing for me. Early evening meant more wireless or even a game of tiddly-winks or shove-halfpenny or bagatelle. Grandad was a great expert at tiddlywinks. I do not remember cards being played at Hornchurch.

Music was so much part of the life of the family. There were two important annual musical events on the wireless which Grandad listened to in their entirety. Just before Christmas Handel's Messiah was performed by the Huddersfield Choral Society with Isobel Baillie as the Soprano Soloist. He felt that she had the finest voice of that range and at both my grandmother Wells and my mother's funeral, the organist played 'I know that My Redeemer Liveth' as the cortege entered the church and the crematorium. At Eastertide he listened to a performance of Stainer's Crucifixion from one of the London Churches. His music has fallen from fashion today but as a Victorian he loved it. One of his favourite songs was the old Music Hall song 'My old Dutch' which he would sing with his tuneful baritone voice to my grandmother. On his wedding anniversary in mid July he would give her a large bunch of cherries. This never varied from year to year throughout the forty-seven years of their marriage. Routine gave security and in a loving relationship can be the basis of a deeper inner bond. I never heard a cross word pass between my grandparents, no doubt they had their moments but they were totally devoted to each other.

It was while I was staying at Hornchurch that I was taken to the Cinema for the first time. I believe we went to Dagenham Heathway by underground and that the cinema was near to that station. The film was Pinocchio and I loved every moment of it. The world of the only child can be a lonely one and it is often necessary to invent imaginary friends and I found it easy to identify with characters in stories, plays or films. The little wooden puppet's desire to be a real boy and to obtain that end fired my fertile imagination. I loved the good Gepito but feared 'Honest John'. The good-fairy's words to Pinocchio to prove yourself 'brave, truthful and unselfish' appealed to my altruistic nature. The antics of Jiminy Cricket, who was Pinocchio's conscience, amused me greatly. Despite being an intense and far too serious child, the latent humour which later became one of my most obvious characteristics was always there.

The dreams of the characters in that fine film were epitomised in the song which has always haunted me. 'When you wish upon a star your dreams come true'. I often made wishes as a child especially at Christmas as I was given the wishbone to break with one of the family. Selflessly they always let me have the bone so that I could have the large part and so make the wish. I remember the excitement of making the wish and really believing that it might come true. It is only as I grew older that I realised that wishes do not often come true and that this world can be a hard, lonely and cruel place. I hate seeing people hurt by the circumstances of their lives. If I could wish today I would like to see the end of selfishness, greed and the exploitation of other people. The heartache and bewilderment of so many can blunt the faith, trust and idealism of youth. It is so easy to become cynical. When I was a teacher working with young children who came to each day with zest, verve and new hope I soon lost any sense of pessimism. Every new day brought a sense of hope. My work as a priest is mostly with the sad, bereaved, and lost people who pass in and out of the valley of the shadow of death, doubt and despair. Much time is spent in discussion of money matters and of maintaining beautiful but old buildings. In the schools today there is a sense that teachers are no longer valued and that they are expected to cope with changes introduced far too quickly and without financial provision.

There are those wonderful moments when you see the true dignity and courage of people which give new hope and make cynicism seem so shallow.

Gran Wells would tell me if I fell over and cut myself and shed tears to "be a brick, like Billy". She knew how to encourage a sensitive and at times fearful child with the right word at the right time. She also had a wonderful way with plants and certainly had "green fingers". The garden at Hornchurch reflected her tender loving care. Her medicine cupboard contained patent medicines for every occasion, When I had a cough she would give me a teaspoon of Galloways Cough Mixture, at Cove Gran Kinsman was a firm believer in the power of Owbridges Cough Mixture. Toothache was treated with Nitre and Gran Well's rheumatics called for vigorous applications of Elliman's Horse Linament or Embrocation. This was applied liberally and her bedroom often smelt strongly of it. If she had a bad headache she would tie up her head in a bandage or scarf. She was a great believer in the power of an aspirin whenever she had a headache not knowing that it also was a means of thinning the blood. She lived to be 86 and enjoyed very good health until almost the end of her long life. The secret of her longevity was her contented nature and the ability to laugh even when things were at their blackest and to see the bright side when others could only see unrelieved darkness. Those magic moments spent at Tregudda meant so much to me.

~ BARRY'S LANE ~

When I was ten and a half years of age we moved from four Coastguard Station, Hawkers Cove, where I was born, to live in Padstow. This does not mean that I lost contact with Cove, as we frequently walked there to visit Gran and Aunty Kath. There were a number of reasons for this move. Grandad Wells had retired, after fifty-one years service, from his office at Samuel Hanson's in Eastcheap. My grandparents were quite anxious to move to Cornwall as they realised that my mother would never leave the Padstow area to live in London. The great love which they had of Cornwall drew them to spend the last years of their lives in the surroundings they most enjoyed. I was approaching the age when children sat the Scholarship examination (not yet called the eleven plus) and if I was successful it would have been very difficult to reach Padstow to catch the 8.10am train to Bodmin and it would be 5.00pm before the train arrived back at Padstow. There would then be a further journey to Cove. My mother needed to work full-time and was cycling six miles each day to and from work.

Our house at Cove never held the warmth for me that I felt for either the Pilots house or for Tregudda. This was strange because it was my birthplace and residence for the first ten and a half years of my life. The house had associations of sadness for my mother. It was where she endured her bereavement silently, spending long hours alone, working hard, going without to ensure that I had the right start in life, and living with her memories of her short but happy marriage. My mother's care, support and selfless love for me were so obvious, yet while she remained there she must have suffered intensely wrestling stoically with the succession of blows which life dealt her. The inward grief of so private a person was deep, the scars of the loss of the only love of her life permanent. She suffered in lonely silence, unable to share this heavy burden with others. She could not show her emotions. Her tears did not flow as easily as the Kinsman family who were, as Aunty Lu often said, 'watery-eyed'. No doubt she did shed tears alone but they were kept from others and, above all, from me.

The move to Padstow opened up a new world for me. My grandparents sold their bungalow in Hornchurch and bought an early Victorian, slate-hung, detached house in Barry's Lane. It bore the name of 'Rhodesia' called by a former owner, Capt. Mark Bate, after his boat of that name which traded with Rhodesia. The house was set back from the road, with a small garden at the front and side of it. The double-fronted dwelling faced south and on each side of the front door were two sizeable reception rooms with flat-roofed bays. One served as my grandparents' sitting and dining room, the other as our lounge. Behind these rooms, leading off the hall, were a kitchen and back kitchen. The kitchen was shared by the ladies who cooked on the electric stove. An Ideal boiler heated the hot water and warmed the room. We ate our meals there. At first the cooking was a joint activity, but as my grandmother grew older my mother took over the cooking. The stone-floored back kitchen was a 'glory hole' where all kinds of objects were stored.

There were three bedrooms, two of which had their own wash basin. The bathroom was a converted bedroom reached by descending three steps, and leading off this was the upstairs loo. My grandparents slept in the bedroom nearest the bathroom as they had no wash-basin in that room. The largest bedroom, which had three very sizeable sash windows, was my mothers. I had the smallest but warmest bedroom, over the kitchen, which also contained the airing cupboard. This was the family home until 1980 when my mother and I moved to St. Issey Old Vicarage. I lived at home until I started training to be a teacher at Culham College of Education in 1959 and returned home to live in 1966 when I became Headmaster of St. Issey School. My grandfather Wells died at 'Rhodesia' in 1957 and Gran Wells in 1972.

The move to Padstow took place in March 1951, which meant that I had just over a term left of my Primary schooling. The last term at Padstow Primary School was a particularly happy one as I made so many more friends. During the ensuing summer evening I played cricket either in Rainyfields, now, sadly, built on, or at the top of Chapel Stile Field. We were also able to watch the water-polo matches held in the inner quay when the evening spring tides filled it. We sat on the edge of the quay dangling our legs over the quayside.

~ PADSTOW SCHOOL ~

Padstow School was a typical Cornish Board School designed by Silvanus Trevail, who was the Architect of so many Board Schools which mushroomed after the Forster Education Act of 1870. The buildings were strongly made, with large, high windows placed above the level of the pupils gaze so avoiding possible distraction from the hard work which was expected of the Victorian child. The classrooms had high ceilings and were well ventilated. The School stood near to the top of the main hill out of the town which was always known in my childhood as "School Board Hill" although the street was actually called New Street. It was opened in 1876, and for generations children of this tight-Knit community received their education there. For most of its history it was an all-age School catering for all the children of the town. The opening of Bodmin County School, known as "Harleigh" to the local people, following the 1902 Act meant that the children who passed the Scholarship and whose families could afford the uniform and train fares left at eleven. In 1957 Wadebridge Secondary Modern School opened, which meant that Padstow became a Primary School. This fine old building ceased to be a school in July, 1988, when the spacious new County Primary School replaced it. The old building has been made into houses, while in the grounds are built three rows of modern cottages. I now live in one of them. No more is it alive with the sound of children shouting excitedly in the playground or of the chanting of the multiplication tables which we did each morning as children. Although it was built as a single building it was originally three schools, an Infant School, a Girls' School, and a Boys' each with their own Head Teacher. The Girls and Infant School were amalgamated well before I started there but it was not until 1949 that it became a single school. I well remember the rumour which became fact that when Miss Ninham, the last head of the Girls School, retired, Mr. Ashbee, the then Head of the Boys, would become Head of the single school.

The transition from home to school can be a traumatic experience for children, especially for an only child like me. I had formed a clear picture of what I believed school to be like before my first day there. My mother had succeeded in instilling favourable attitudes to it. I did not start school until about a month before my sixth birthday. She had refused to send me until transport was provided for we lived over three miles from the school. For many years the children of Hawkers Cove had walked in all weathers to school often arriving soaked to the skin and chilled to the bone. These were not ideal conditions in which to begin the school day. The Education Act of 1944 had made the local Education Authority responsible for providing transport for children living three miles from the school and for children under eight two miles.

I never saw the correspondence which took place between my mother and the then Secretary for Education but eventually it was agreed to provide a school car to take the children of Hawkers Cove to and from school each day.

Padstow had a long history of schools of various kinds, well before the First Great Education Act of 1870. The earliest was probably that maintained by the trustees of the Revd Sir John Elliot's charitable Trust who endowed schools with £5 per annum which provided five free places for scholars.

The National Society gave grants to help establish a school in High Street above the entrance to the Marble Arch. This narrow passage, way so unlike its prestigious name sake in London, runs from High Street down into Church Street ending with a steep flight of steps under a cottage which protrudes into the latter street.

The school was built in 1819/20 along with a workhouse underneath. In the usual way, public sub-scriptions were sought and obtained to complete the work. In the large classroom, measuring 50' x 25', children were taught using the monitorial system of Dr. Bell. This system allowed a large number of pupils to be educated by a single teacher who instructed monitors, who then, in turn, taught the children. The methods were simple and the learning was all by rote. It was cheap to operate and so highly favoured by the then leaders of educational thought.

The school was originally a mixed school but as numbers increased the Girls and Infants were transferred to a school converted from a dwelling house at the top of Ruthy's Lane. The Prideaux-Brune family maintained the building there and took a keen interest in the education of the children of the town.

One of the principal aims of Victorian Education was to produce children who could read, write and do simple arithmetic. The Boys National School certainly did this and had a fine reputation for the copper-plate handwriting of its pupils. Handwriting was once cynically described as the dunce's accom-plishment. The Victorians spent hours practising this cursive hand in their copy books. The thin and thick strokes of each letter were meticulously observed as vigorously as the "law of the Medes and Persians which altereth not".

By the time I attended Primary School, Cursive writing had been replaced by a much simpler style known as Marion Richardson's which was nearer to the type used in reading.

Marion Richardson was the originator of this type of writing and of the writing patterns which were associated with it. It strenuously avoided the use of loops. I do not remember having formal handwriting lessons as such, indeed, my handwriting as a child was spidery and irregular. I found it very difficult to write as quickly as I thought and my muscular co-ordination was poor. Many a time, as I sat at my desk in school, my mind was moving far ahead of the word or sentence I was writing as the next idea flashed across my mind. I was not good at routine tasks which led me to be labelled, very fairly, as impractical by nature.

One of the many private schools kept by a series of great characters, probably with very little educational knowledge but compensated for by a delightful degree of eccentricity, was kept by Mr. Philip Trescowthick. He lived at Crugmeer where he had a boys school which was held in the evenings in his kitchen Later he kept a small school in Church Street in Padstow. His main occupation was that of a tombstone maker and engraver. Many of the fine headstones in Padstow Churchyard bear his name. Philip could not manage his money and when he had some cash in his pocket he would often become very drunk. After a bout of tippling he had to return through the lanes in his donkey cart. It was a good job that the animal knew its way home. His poor wife Elizabeth, was naturally angry when he arrived home. She had the difficult task of persuading him to go to bed. His usual retort to this plea was to threaten to jump down the well near their cottage. The boys attending his school learned Algebra, which was then considered to be a sign of a good education.

Another of these schools was that of William Brown, who was also the Post Master. The original Post Office was in Church Street opposite the Church Rooms. This school was mixed, but the boys and girls were separated by a partition while being instructed. When the afternoon mail arrived the girls were sent into the kitchen while it was sorted. Scholars attending this school learnt French which, like Algebra was considered to be a suitable accomplishment by the upwardly mobile Victorian Middle Classes.

Perhaps the most attractive setting for a school was in a room below the sail loft near to the Custom House where boys, including William Berry, had their education. William was the father of that greatly loved son of Padstow, Claude Berry, who for many years was editor of the West Briton. The playground was the nearby foreshore and beach. The quality of these early private and day schools varied greatly and the gradual emergence of Universal education was a result of great efforts by the National Society, and British and Foreign Schools Society. The National Society, which thought to teach children in the principles of education according to the Anglican Church, and the British Schools, whose education was inter-denominational but Bible-based, both had schools in Padstow.

Unlike many towns in Cornwall there was no battle between the Church of England and the local Board School. The National Society handed over its existing schools from the formation of the school board in 1873. The Headmaster appointed by the Board for the Boys School became the first headmaster of the newly built boys school when it opened in 1876. Boss Harding, as he was affectionately known, must have found it a great cultural shock when he, as a young man, came to his first and only Headship. F. G. Harding, a teacher of the second class trained at St. Mark's College at Chelsea, entered a tough and tight-knit community.

Many boys deeply resented having to attend school, as did their parents, who were anxious in those times, often of great poverty, to receive the small wages a boy could earn. He had to establish a good reputation for the school and gain trust from the parents, who were suspicious and often antagonistic to education. He had to ensure a sufficient number of the pupils reached certain standards in the basic curriculum to qualify for the government grant. James Udy (1828-1908), an Uncle of my great-grandmother, Mary Wood- Hooper (1850-1925) kept an earthenware and grocer's shop in the Lanadwell St. and was also a Postman and Barber in Padstow during the last quarter of the 19th century. This was often a time of great hardship. He could read fluently and was a great Radical. It was he who read the news from the daily papers to those who could not read. His strongly liberal views would have appreciated the need for people to be able to read for themselves and so not be dominated by the views of the more privileged classes of the town. Boss Harding opened the Boys Board School on the 26th June, 1873. The Board had decided upon a sliding scale for pupils attending the school. If there were one or two children in a family, the fees were threepence a week, three or four, twopence, five, a penny Ha' penny, and six or over, a penny. The church school at nearby St. Issey charged all the children two pence a week. It was a Herculean task imparting knowledge to a community where much poverty and a sturdy independence were in evidence. The early log book shows the problem of late-comers and truancy to be rife. The entry for the 27th June, 1873 was typical. 'The pupils that had come for the most part, very late, and the little ones are especially very restless'. 'Truancy was very common', he writes, with a certain degree of sadness, on the 22nd July of that same year. 'I have had a good deal of trouble with one or two boys playing truant from time to time'.

The parents wanted the children to be earning their pittances to supplement the family income. Children were employed in picking stones for which they received two pence a day. Some of the older Padstow-nians of my childhood days talked of this and remembered working in the deer park opposite Prideaux Place doing just that. The Harvest Season caused truancy to rise and on the fourth of August, 1873 he writes in desperation 'There are two boys, Henry Irons and George Dale, still much given to playing truant. The former especially seems almost incorrigible, he is nine years old and does not know a letter. Their parents ought to be made to send their boys to school'.

The workhouse below had its effect on the school curriculum, for in consequence of one of the inmates of the dwellings beneath the school being very ill there was no singing lesson on the afternoon of the 18th February,1874. There was wide-spread ignorance about education and a certain degree of gullibility. Poor Boss Harding was suffering from being compared with Mr. Isaacs the previous Head. It is strange that in public life you often acquire a degree of sanctification after your leave a post. He pours out his deep feelings in the entry made on the 20th January, 1875. 'Many of the parents who are ignorant themselves think their children have arrived in a high degree of scholarship if the children have managed to read some easy paragraphs tolerably correctly. The reading too is generally a wretched sing-song. As an instance of the ridiculous ideas which I believe are not in common with scholastic matters in Padstow, I could quote the substance of a dialogue which took place between Nicholls, the pupil teacher, and an insignificant keeper of a small school in the town. He heard that we, in this school, had dictation four times one day. "Dictation's not any good, Mr. Isaacs, who used to keep school here, never used to have Dictation and he turned out some very good scholars"'

The school was adversely affected by pupils absences at the time of examinations. The headmaster comments sarcastically on the poor attendance on the day of the drawing examination on the 8th March

1874. 'Seven boys were sent stone-picking, many of the boys seem eagerly to run from school on this examination day to pursue the intellectual employment of stone-picking .

Of course these stone-pickers were among the lowest class of the children. They were, as I afterwards told them, 'the ones most likely to become stone crackers on the road to their old age while others among them might aspire to important positions.' Major events in the town, like the return of Lieutenant Brune from the Ashantee war of the 8th April,1874 closed the school. It was May Day which came in for the head teacher's most scathing comments. "On the other hand, May Day in Padstow, when almost every other city, town and village is in its usual working order, is a season of rejoicing among the lower classes beyond ridiculous." Good Frederick Harding was perplexed by the intense fervour in which May day was celebrated, and is celebrated and always be celebrated. There was, however, improvement, for which he can justifiably take credit. The school held a concert at the end of the Autumn Term 1877 and he writes, with the pride that a dedicated teacher has, when this happened 'Some of the boys sang alto and the impulse given has awakened an interest for singing such as I have never seen here before.

'On the 19th October, 1880, the boys in the fifth and sixth standard seem to be taking a great interest in "The Merchant of Venice" and to be improving in their composition.'

These were in the early days of the boy's school but my Aunt talked about the girl's school and especially the diminutive, but capable and rigid Kate Bailey. She was head teacher at Padstow Girl's School for well over 20 years. Her reputation spread far and wide and undoubtedly had a profound effect on the school. It was particularly successful with its choir and won numerous competitions under her musical direction. Aunty Beat, who had a very sallow skin, was made to wash her neck regularly on arrival at school by Kate Bailey. She had the indignity of having another girl supervise this. The problem was not dirt, which found no place in her home, but her particularly yellow skin. My grandmother abhorred dirt and her children were sent to school clean as a new pin. One of the most vivid memories of my aunt's school days was an incident which involved an irate mother dragging Kate Bailey around the girls playground by her hair. The sheer horror and audacity of this incident left a permanent mark on her school-girl memories. They told me, as I grew older and questioned them about their childhood, how children in their classes who were left-handed had their left hands firmly tied behind their backs while they were made to write with their right hand. Schools were then places of total conformity of behaviour and ideas. I was thankful that when I received my education, creativity and original thought were encouraged.

Sewing and knitting formed part of the girls curriculum. My aunts would joke about having to mend Kate's bloomers. No doubt they were the kind which were conveniently referred to as Passion Killers. Kate's passion went into her teaching, to which she was completely dedicated.

There were no school dinners then and the children from Cove had to carry their own with them. My grandmother would make beautiful pasties, which were easy to carry, for their lunches. There was no question of the children not being well-fed despite limited money. She would rather go without her own dinner than see the children short.

The girls had cooking lessons in the small room in Fentonluna Lane which later served as a Guide room. They would walk from the Board School to be taught by Miss Olive, who ran a Boarding House at Trevone. Miss Olive was a delightful person, who lived well into her nineties - her father had, at one time, been Vicar of Warleggan. She had that natural courtesy and bearing which daughters of the clergy were expected to show in Victorian times. During one of the interregnums I took her communion regularly and, after she had received her communion, I listened to her recalling the days of her childhood. Just before my sixth birthday I started school. It was in July 1946, and only three weeks remained of the school year. The emotions which I, an only child, felt were very mixed. I was entering a world where I would need to share the time of the teacher with others. I was timid and apprehensive yet anxious to please and avoid being reprimanded. My first teacher was Miss Betty Chidgey ,a kind but firm Reception Class Teacher. I was only in her class until the end of the term as I had missed the rest of the year. I should have been there. It was fortunate that I could read and handle simple arithmetical calculations. I well remember that first morning. The anxious wait for the car to come and pick me up along with the other children from Hawkers Cove. I gather that my education began in earnest well before I reached school and by the end of the first week at school I had learned certain words which I had never used before and was even able to sing the sad story of three old ladies who were unfortunately locked in the lavatory. If I was to be believed they were there from Monday to Saturday and their absence was never noticed. My mother related this incident to one of her friends who was worried about her child who had newly started school coming home using bad language. She told her not to worry as I had done the same. The reception class was situated in the largest classroom in the Girls and Infant School which

Padstow Board School - later Padstow County Primary School

later became the Hall. We sat on tiny round chairs with arms and played with plasticine, which smelt strongly. I had a habit of smelling all the food I ate as a child and my sense of smell was acute. Each day began with an assembly for the infants. We sang hymns which I later learnt were from Carey Bonner collection for schools. "Jesus friend of little children", "All Things Bright and Beautiful" and "Gentle Jesus Meek and Mild" were among them. One of the favourite hymns was 'Sing a Song of May Time' which was also sung at the children's May Festival at the Parish Church. Its popularity was due to its associations with Padstow May Day rather than because of the words it contained. Carey Bonner's hymns were still sung in the Infant Department of Padstow School when I acted as a Teacher Helper at Padstow County Primary School in 1958-59.

Playtime was preceded by the drinking of milk. I hated milk and did not have it, although on occasions I was encouraged to do so. At playtime we played in the large Girls and Infants yard at the back of the school. The toilets, or offices were set at the far side of the yard. In classtime we had to ask if we could use them. In the Boys School there was a set routine. You put up your hand and on being asked what you wanted said 'Please Sir, may I go to the Office?' The Boys Infant Urinal and Boys Junior Urinal bore little resemblance to any other. They were exposed to all wind and weather although there was a degree of shelter in the Infant one. The wind whistled around the Urinal and the rain beat down on your head. A small child would become very wet running across the playground to them. Perhaps this acted as a deterrent and stopped unnecessary time wasting.

The senior girls, who shared the hard surfaced yard, played various ball games or singing games such as "the Big Ship sails through the Ally-Ally-O" or "Oranges and Lemons" during their break. There was a large air raid shelter near to one of the walls, for it had not yet been taken down when I was in the Infant Classes. The yard was flanked by a highish wall which separated it from the Head Teacher's house next door. In that garden there were apple trees from which apples were known to have been surreptitiously stolen.

The surface of the playground was hard and children who fell over often received grazed knees or elbows. These would be bathed, with a diluted Dettol solution, by one of the teachers or the older girls (who remained at school up to fourteen years of age at that time).

I spent very little time in the Infant School as my mother went to London to work for the winter which followed my starting school. We stayed with her parents at Hornchurch and I attended Sutton Lane Primary School there.

When I transferred to the Boys School in the September after my seventh birthday my education began in earnest. The boys of Padstow school were tough and needed firm handling. The teacher of that lower Junior Class was a Mr. Yole, who had a large moustache and maintained order with frequent application of a small cane with a knob on. Hardly a lesson went by without one of the boys being caned on the hand.

I could read fluently by this time and was therefore useful when we had group reading, which was then very much in vogue. The stories in the Group Readers included those of the Heroes of Ancient Greece, which I greatly enjoyed but which left many of the boys totally bored and did not encourage them to read fluently.

The desks in the small classroom, which later became the School Staff Room, were closely packed together and you sat at an iron desk for two on a seat to be lifted to allow your companion to reach his place. Between the desks, which were placed in straight rows, was a narrow gangway along which passed the penitent or hardened offender for the cane. The teacher's desk was placed at the front of the class and was next to the blackboard and easel. In the ledges of the high windows were geranium plants which seemed to flower very infrequently and had a rather unpleasant smell. The walls were, for the most part, bare, although the multiplication tables were displayed for learning. Each morning we chanted them with a sing-song intonation beginning with the two times table 'Once two is two, two twos are four, and ending with twelve twelves are one hundred and forty-four'. The rooms echoed with the lilt of the chanting. This ritual followed the Scripture lesson. We would often hear neighbouring classes following the same routine. I joined in although I found it rather tedious as I knew my tables and had made my own table book at home with tables up to the twenty times.

Each morning there was an Assembly for the Boys School in the larger classrooms across the stone passageway which led to the Head Teachers Room. A large screen separating these two rooms was drawn back making it into a kind of hall. We were packed tightly into these rooms. The pattern of worship never varied, although each day of the week had its own particular Service with a hymn or two hymns, prayers and responses. The Service which, was a mini liturgy, was taken from the Daily Service Book which was in use in most Primary Schools from the mid 1930's until the end of the 1960's. The little service and hymn books were very tatty, and I seem to remember that some hymns were written up on large sheets at the front of the room. The hymns were sung with gusto. There was no pianist in the Junior Boys School and until our class became mixed. Mr. Ashbee would strike the first note with a tuning fork and the boys would bellow out the first line of the hymn. Some of the older boys sang cautiously as their voices had broken.

Boys of fifteen, already anxiously waiting to leave school and earn their first pay packet, were often silent while we sang 'Glad that I live am I'. One of Mr. Ashbee's favourite hymns was that great hymn of John Bunyan 'He who would Valiant Be.'

Mr. Ashbee was a firm disciplinarian but one of the fairest men that I have ever met. He was a great influence on me as a young boy. We were in awe of him yet there was a bond and respect which developed because of his complete justice. He could use his supple cane with telling power on the older boys.

They were caned, if the offence was serious enough, in front of the whole school. The miscreant had to bend over and touch his toes while the cane swished through the air and landed with a massive thwack on the bottom.

In the large classroom which served as a Hall were cases of wild, stuffed birds, many of them sea birds, who looked down from their glass enclosure on generations of school children.

Each of the classrooms was fronted by a Tortoise Stove with the motto on 'Slow but sure combustion'. A large guard enclosed the stove and by the side of it was a large pail or hod full of coke which was filled each day by the caretaker. The teacher would sometimes ask one of the senior boys to fill up the stove when it needed to be replenished. A young child does not feel the cold but I am pretty certain that it was only those in close proximity who felt the full benefit of the stove. When the teacher was out of the room I have seen boys spit on the hot top of it to produce a sizzling noise.

After morning Assembly we had our Scripture lessons, which were mainly bible based and related to the life of Jesus. The various festivals of the Church were given prominence, although care was always taken not to show denominational bias. Mr. Ashbee was a keen Churchman who became Church-Warden towards the end of his career at the school. Mr. Derek Grubb, who taught me for the last two years at Junior School was a practising Methodist. The Miracles and Parables of Jesus were taught and I can remember being told on a number of occasions, that a Parable was an earthly story with a heavenly meaning. I also remember Mr. Grubb telling us about Wilfrid Grenfell and his missionary work in Labrador. I cannot remember learning any passages of scripture off by heart.

After Scripture it was time to recite the multiplication tables and then to have, on most days, Mental Arithmetic. I loved this as I found it easy to make instant calculations in my head. I rarely failed to obtain full marks in this. The Arithmetic lesson was another favourite of mine. The sums were written on a blackboard placed on an easel at the front of the classroom. I quickly romped through them and was soon at the teacher's desk to have them marked. I was crestfallen if I was sent back to do a correction for I hated having a sum marked with a cross, indicating that it was wrong. As I worked out most of the sums in my head it was difficult to persuade me to show the necessary workings in my exercise book. The sums were nearly always right but it would be untruthful to say that they were tidily presented. There were often small blots made by picking up some of the blotting paper and remnants of the ink, which I believe was made from powder in large ink containers. Monitors were sent out to the cloakroom on occasions to wash out the ink-well and also, I believe, to make up the ink. The problem for me was time. My mind raced through the calculations and I was anxious to finish first. The routine care needed to present neat work did not accord with the frenetic pace of my life.

Arithmetic lasted until the mid-morning break and first playtime. Before play the children who had milk were given their third of a pint of milk to drink and the monitors took the empty crate away to wash up at the beginning of the break.

In winter the boys played football in the yard. The game was intense and rather rough and often interrupted by minor fights which seemed to be a feature of those playtimes. I did not care much for the rough and tumble of the football. In the summer, however, it was cricket which took over. I loved cricket and in the summer of 1951 played with the Senior boys developing the ability to make the soft rubber ball turn. My slow leg-breaks puzzled some of them and I had a crop of wickets. I had learned how to bowl leg-breaks from the Eagle comic which I had each week. I spent hours tweaking the ball against the wall in the yard of the Coastguard House at Hawker's Cove. My batting was not so successful and I did not relish the games of cricket played with a proper cricket ball when a fast bowler sent the ball thundering towards me.

In the autumn we played Conkers. Boys soaked their conkers in vinegar to harden them and conkers were exchanged for Marbles, which was also played in the yard. Although I was a gentle, and rather timid, child I was never bullied by the older boys who were often quite protective towards me when they played cricket with me. Padstow was a tough community but underneath the aggressive exterior there was a great deal of care and kindness.

In the second half of the morning there was usually some form of English. It may have been a 'Composition'. Some of the titles of the compositions set were those which generations of children had written about. The Life Story of a Penny allowed scope to the imaginative child to present his knowledge of the production of coins from the Mint to the pocket of a child. I collected pennies from the reign of Queen Victoria. It fascinated me to see the change which took place in the head of Queen Victoria from her young life, when she had her hair in a bun, to the coins from the end of her long reign when she was veiled.

We had regular Spelling tests and also Dictation. We did simple exercises in basic grammar and punctuation. At the end of morning school we sang Grace. It was nearly always the traditional one, 'Be Present at Our Table Lord'. We stood behind our desks while singing this. The children who lived in Padstow were then dismissed and allowed to go home for their dinner. Those who stayed at school were then escorted, in crocodile file, to the School Canteen, which was between a quarter and half a mile away. The Canteen was built at the end of the last war and catered for midday meals until the new school was opened in 1988. I did not like school dinners but this was not a criticism of the meals but of my faddy eating habits. I was a nightmare to feed. My poor mother was often at her wits end trying to encourage me to eat more. My grandmother Kinsman, who had reared seven children who ate well, even asked her if she was feeding me properly.

The dinner hour lasted from 12 noon until 1.30pm. There was time before and after dinner to play cricket in summer or just to talk to friends in the school playground. The school, being situated near to the top of the hill, was very exposed and the wind and rain swept across the yard in squalls in winter. In summer it became very warm and the ground was hot to sit on. The surface of the yard was very uneven and there was always a crop of grazed and cut knees.

At one-thirty the whistle was blown. This meant that you stood still wherever you were in the yard. A deep silence descended where a moment before the yard was the scene of noisy children playing. This was followed by a second blast on the whistle and you ran to the appropriate line of children who formed up opposite the entrance to the passage leading to the classroom. 'Stand at ease', bellowed the teacher on duty, followed by 'Attention' and 'Right Turn'. The children then filed silently into the classroom. This routine was followed at the beginning of school and after the morning and afternoon playtimes. Any child who talked in lines was punished. School began in silence. At the beginning of each session the register was called and you were expected to say 'Present'. In the morning this was followed by the collection of dinner money.

Afternoon school was devoted to such activities as P.E., Art, Handwork, Games, or Music. P.E. was largely confined to the summer months as there was no hall. The lesson was of the standard type with exercises for basic parts of the body followed by various teams games and relays. We were divided into four teams; red, green, yellow and blue. We wore our respective coloured bands. Fierce competition raged between the colours. We ran over-the-legs relays, passed a football between our legs from front to back of the team, or weaved our way in and out of the other members of the team suitably spaced for this activity. In winter, when you spent hours in the class-room occasionally we played games such as 'O'Grady says do this' but there was little scope to let off steam.

The Art lessons were mainly painting, using powder paints which were mixed thickly and used directly on to quite small pieces of paper. Jars of water were given out by the monitors. It was a rare occasion when an Art lesson passed without at least one of them being knocked over by a clumsy child, causing a stream to flow across the classroom floor. There were the other streams which flowed, more especially in Infant Classes, when a child wet itself either through fear of asking to go to the office or because he had some bladder problems. I disliked Art, as I could not draw or paint well. I have often wondered why this is as I have a very observant eye and enjoy looking at great paintings. I suspect that it needed the time and patience which I did not have. I wanted instant results.

The history lessons were wonderful to me. The world of the great Explorers, the names of the Rulers of England and the events which enthralled the nation enthralled me. I had a book at home called 'Our

Island Story' which I read and re-read through the years of my childhood. I loved that book and the Whittaker's Almanac which my grandfather had with a complete list of the Kings of England. In his bookcase at Hornchurch was Green's History of England which contained a much more detailed account of the history of this nation. I would spend hours reading this when staying there.

In the third year of the Junior School we sat the Preliminary Examinations which preceded the Scholarship Examination which determined whether you went to Bodmin Grammar School or remained at Padstow School. The Preliminary contained an essay and I remember that I wrote about the history of Padstow while in the actual examination, a year later, I wrote about a Country Walk.

Two managers came into the school to assist with the supervision of the exams. They were the then County Councillor, Mr. William Tamblyn Kestell, and Mr. Charlie Major. The Arithmetic Paper caused me no real difficulty and I finished well before the end of the time. The Intelligence Test took me longer to complete. I remember little about the English Paper. There had been some talk about me sitting the Scholarship a year earlier but as I had an August birthday this would have meant that I would have only been 10 when I went to the Grammar School. I was not emotionally mature enough to cope at that age.

We moved to Padstow in March 1951 and it was about that time that I sat the final examinations. My mother was then working at Eustaces Cafe' which was situated on the Quay. The results of the exam were announced to the whole school. Six of us passed, four girls and two boys. We were then allowed

Myself at Padstow School

72

to go home and tell our respective families the good news. I ran fleet-footed down School Bound Hill and was completely breathless when I arrived at the 'Cafe'. My mother was puzzled to see me, but delighted when I told her the news. 'I've passed, I've passed for Bodmin' I excitedly told her. My grandparents Wells had moved from London to live with us at the same time we had left Hawkers Cove and so I then ran to Barry's Lane, where we now lived. The proud grandparents were then given the same news.

But what of those who had not passed? I felt so sorry for them. Many of my friends had been promised bicycles or watches if they were successful. I had passed, but there was no present dependent on an exam for me. I was given a watch on my eleventh birthday which was promised whether I passed or not. I gather that Mr. Ashbee had told my mother that I would almost certainly go to the Grammar School. The last term at Padstow School was one of the happiest of my school days. Mr. Derek Grubb, who was a good and wise teacher, allowed me to spend much time on a project on Padstow which I chose to do. Old Post Cards and some of my grandfather's photographs were used in my mini history of Padstow which I wrote in my spidery uneven handwriting. I looked at the Guide Book to Padstow which then contained some of the history of the town and read Claude Barry's "Cornwall", in which Padstow so largely features. My love of history and of writing and researching was given the right impetus at the opportune moment. How valuable this was to me. The consuming interest of my leisure time and the intense satisfaction of piecing together the history of my beloved Padstow began in earnest then and will continue until I am no longer able to do any further research.

At this distance of time, as I reflect on this life-long interest, I have often wondered why local history means so much to me. I am naturally curious, indeed, some would say nosy.

People are very important to me. I love the variety of human beings and their idiosyncrasies. The great characters of the past, especially the human events of their lives, are easily linked to my own. I have the ability to empathise with others and stand in their shoes. It has never been difficult for me to enter into the joys and sorrows of others. I have found it much more difficult to distance myself from situations. It has not been easy for me to stop myself from becoming emotionally involved with others in their lives. Curiosity, an active mind, deep emotions, and a sense of the past, only partially explains this interest and enthusiasm. The sense of belonging to a community gives me security, and it is to Padstow and Cove that I belong. The wider community is my family, as were my parishioners at St. Issey and Little Petherick. The angels and archangels of the past are not vague ethereal creatures but real people, often flawed like myself, who have become part of my story and that of the community I was privileged to grow up in.

~ THE PARISH CHURCH ~

On Easter Day we attended Evensong at Padstow Parish Church. This fine, mainly fifteenth century Church built largely during the Wars of the Roses and containing portions of the earlier Norman Church stands on the site of the first church, which was the monastery St. Petroc founded, was full. It was my first experience of a huge congregation and of a fine, robed choir, with an extremely talented Organist, leading the singing. I knew the service of Evensong well from my regular attendance at Cove Church but the beauty of a well-sung Evensong ending with a procession around the church, filled with me a sense of the presence of God. The order, dignity, and sheer beauty of the service, opened up a new dimension in my life.

We sung a hymn that has become one of my particular favourites. 'Thine Be the Glory' to a tune from Judas Maccabeus, one of Handel's well-known Oratorios, where the Air is sung to the words 'See the Conquering Hero Comes'. When I became a choirboy, soon after moving to Padstow, I quickly learnt other words to it.

At the Annual Padstow Regatta which, until the last war, took place as part of the Whitsuntide feast celebrations, this piece of music was played by the band as the winning boat crossed the finishing line.

There were two boats, the" Annie" and the "Silver Spray", which usually took a number of prizes. When they were victorious the crowd would sing:

"Way goes the Annie,
She hath got the prize,
None of the boats in the harbour
Could beat her for her size".

or supporters of the Silver Spray would sing the same verse substituting" Silver Spray" for" Annie". These words were irrevently sung by some of the choirboys as the hymn was being sung by the congregation.

The influence of Padstow Church on my life was profound. Just after Easter I joined the choir and attended the Sunday School held on Sunday afternoon in the Parish Church. This was actually termed 'Catechism' on the Church Notice Board. The Revd. Philip Slocombe used the Prayer Book Catechism as the basis of his addresses at this service when, he skillfully taught the rudiments of the Christian Faith to upwards of 100 boys and girls.

There were two choir practices a week for the choirboys, for there were no girls in the choir then. The choir consisted of about sixteen choirboys, eight men, five soprano ladies, and five contralto ladies. The females were placed in the back row of the choir stalls on either side of the chancel and were not robed. They quietly made their way to their respective places and did not walk with the men choristers, choirboys and servers, in the procession from the choir vestry at the back of the Church.

On Monday evening at six the boys had their practice. We were not allowed into church until the arrival of the organist and choirmaster. He was always known to generations of choirboys as 'Willie Ravenhill', although his Christian names were actually Sidney Marshall. He had come to Padstow for health reasons, just before the outbreak of the First World War. He had formerly been the assistant organist under Charles Lloyd at Gloucester Cathedral. Padstow was lucky to have an organist of such great ability. When I became a choirboy he was already in his late sixties and in very indifferent health following a major operation, probably a colostomy.

'Willie's coming shouted the choir boys and we were then able to follow him into church down the three steps from the North Door. Choir practice began with scale practice and for the first ten minutes we sang 'Coo-coo-coo' or 'La la la' as our clear treble voices climbed and descended the scale. Often the boys were late and so missed that part of the practice. The choirboys of Padstow Church, who looked so angelic in their mauve or purple cassocks, white surplices, and starched white ruffs, were often far from angelic during choir practice. Mr. Ravenhill's gruff voice was often raised to shout at the offender. Paper darts made from old hymn sheets, peas from shooters, and other missiles often crossed the chancel while he sat at the organ looking intently in his mirror to spot the source of the flying object.

Choir practice had a set pattern. When the scales were duly competed, the hymns for the Sunday were practiced. The morning hymns from the English Hymnal were sung first. We had to sing most of the verses to make sure that we knew them thoroughly. The morning service, which was at eleven o'clock on Sunday morning, was either Choral Eucharist the first and third Sunday, or Matins on the other Sundays. The evening service, at six o'clock, was always Evensong. The evening hymns, were from 'Hymns Ancient and Modern Standard Edition', except for the first Sunday when the English Hymnal was used. This typical Anglican compromise stemmed from the attempt of the Revd. Philip Slocombe to introduce the English Hymnal. Mr. Ravenhill preferred the music of the Victorian composers and, I suspect, was rather reluctant to use the English Hymnal. I was lucky to experience such a wide selection of hymns as a choirboy in a small town parish Church.

Many of the hymns were different from those sung in the Mission Church at Cove. I encountered for the first time some of the beautiful Eucharistic hymns of the Church. I had not attended a Eucharist until I moved to Padstow. The beauty of that service soon made it a particular favourite of mine. I much preferred it to Matins. There was a real sense of the otherness of God in this service and of the dramatic and visual impact of the ritual which accompanied it, namely the beauty of the six tall, lighted candles flickering majestically on the high altar and the movement of the congregation quietly to the altar to receive their Communion added to the dignity. It was only the older people who received Communion at the Sung Eucharist, the younger ones were expected to go to the early service to make their communion. Many of the elderly people had been brought up in the days when the Revd. E. F. Nugent was Vicar and had been schooled in the Tractarian tradition. They approached the altar with reverence and also with a deep sense of the real presence of God. There is a deep serenity in an aged face, particularly one whose faith has been sustained by a life time of feeding on 'the Body and Blood of Christ'. While the Communion took place we were expected to kneel and sing the verses of the Communion hymn which was sung one verse at a time with soft music between each verse.

After the hymns were practiced we moved on to the psalms. We had to sing all the verses of the Psalms so that we had the pointing correct. We had our small black pointed psalter - the word edition of the Old Cathedral Psalter. The Psalms seemed long, I think we still sang all the Psalms for the particular day of the month. This was the most boring part of choir practice. One of the psalms I liked best was Psalm 114 'When Israel came out of Egypt' sung on Easter Day evening. Certain verses were sung by the trebles while the basses and tenors sang others. 'What aileth Thee, oh Thou sea, that Thou fleddest', and 'Thou Jordan that Thou wast driven back', boomed out the men. I can still hear the bass's deep voices behind us singing that particular verse.

The second half of the practice was devoted to practising the anthems which were sung at Christmas, Easter, Whitsun and Harvest. We worked on these for weeks in order to get them right. At the practice on Thursday evening we were able to fit our parts with those of the other voices in the choir.

One of the most ambitious anthems we sung was at the special service in Padstow Church for the Coronation of Queen Elizabeth the Second on June 2nd 1953, it was Handel's Zadok the priest. I remember it particularly because of the long runs of music when we sang 'Ah-ah-ah'. The boys practiced these long passages often dissolving into laughter. Ah-ah-ah Amen soon became Ha ha-ha. Mr. Ravenhill, whose fuse was particularly short, became more and more irate as the day for singing the anthem approached.

The church was always bitterly cold for choir practices in the winter. The cold air, so we were told, would produce good singing and often we could see our breath in the chill of a winter's night. The churchyard was pitch black on moonless nights although there was a street light by the North Gate into Church Street. Senior choirboys would tell the younger ones that you could see ghosts if you looked carefully, I hurried home from choir practice when it was winter as I had no desire to see them. By the South East gate of the churchyard was the base of a large Celtic Cross. There was a tradition that if you walked seven times around it and then put your ear to the side of the granite stump you could hear the devil. Many boys did this only to have their head thrust against the hard surface expe-riencing a ringing in the ears made by the impact of the stone.

The bells were rung for the Sunday services every Sunday, and also in the week on Tuesday evening practice was held. The six bells were rehung in 1950 when I was a choirboy and I can remember seeing them on the ground on their return from recasting before they were placed in the tower. The inscrip-tions on the bells fascinated me, the earliest dating from the end of the eighteenth century when John Rudhall of Gloucester was the founder. Muffled peals were rung on Good Friday and Remembrance Sunday and on the anniversary of the death of Nicholas Watts. Watts Knell rang on the 21st of August and would often startle visitors as the town was, at that time, crowded with them. There is a particular beauty in a muffled or half-muffled peal. A single bell tolled as a cortege was taken into the church. In pre-war days, when the Church had a full-time verger, a single bell tolled out the age of the deceased, when it became known they had died. A solitary bell tolling has a great effect on me and I remember those great churchmen and churchwomen of my childhood with affection. It tolled three times for a man, twice for a woman, and once for a child. Then followed a short break before the bell rang the age of the deceased.

There was Annie Bate, with her auburn hair turning grey, and dimpled cheeks, who was the caretaker of the Church and also of the Schoolroom in Ruthy's Lane where small meetings of the Church were held. She was the "essence of kindness' with a deep, simple faith which showed itself in the numerous kindnesses she did for so many people. She spent hours in the church polishing the pews and scrubbing the floor. Each day she would lock and unlock the church with the huge iron key. The church was her life, and her faith her strength. She was warm-hearted and with a great sense of fun. On a grey cold late autumn day when the darkness seemed to creep down in the middle of the afternoon she had a massive stroke while cleaning the church. She lived for a few days but never recovered consciousness. Whenever I hear the parable of the Good Samaritan I think of her.

Her elder son, George, inherited her marvellous disposition. It was his fine strong bass voice which often sang the solos in the anthems. He retained his resonant voice until his death at the age of eighty. He was not only a choirman but also a server and bellringer and, near the end of his life, Church-Warden, and Lay Minister administering the Holy Communion. His memories of the church went back to the First World War. In those days Padstow Church Choir sang the great works of Handel including the "Messiah" and Mendelssohn's "Elijah". They must have had one of the finest parish church choirs in the County. The music I most associate with him is Stainer's "Crucifixion", which was often performed on Good Friday, especially the bass solo 'And as Moses lifteth up the serpent in the wilderness'. This Victorian work was a particular favourite of my grandfather Wells who listened each year to it being performed on the radio. George's wife, Doris, was also a member of the choir with a beautiful, distinctive, contralto voice. She sang solos on various occasions too. She loved the "Messiah" and her rich, deep alto voice was so suited to the contralto solo 'He was despised'. Doris became caretaker of the church after her mother-in-law's death. She was another ministering Angel. All came to her with their troubles, for she had a sympathetic and kind heart. She loved dogs, having a succession of strong dogs who took her for a walk around Stile. Rover, Rex, and Bob were well-known dogs to many Padstownians. On Sunday evenings after Evensong, for many years, I would go to George and Doris's for supper. I loved to hear their memories of church life in former days. It is people like George and Doris with their good practical Christianity who commend the faith to others. When I hear the words from St. Matthew's Gospel 'I was a stranger and ye took me in and naked and I clothed you', I see Doris.

One of the great characters in the choir was May Williams. She lived to be ninety-eight. She was a spinster but had a wicked, and sometimes crude, sense of humour. She wore fine clothes and particularly large hats. She did not know how to put on rouge and her face often looked as if she was being auditioned to be a circus clown. It was on the Choir outings, which took place during the Summer Holidays encouraged by the Vicar the Revd. Philip Slocombe, that we would cheekily sing to the tune of the Quartermasters' store:

"There was May,May,
Her big hat in the way,
In the store, in the store,
There was May, May,
Her big hat in the way,
In the quartermasters' store."

She was a most faithful member of the church, always in her seat in the row of sopranos for each service. She also played the piano for the Kindergarten Sunday School which met each Sunday morning in the Church Rooms. One of the last memories I have of her was on a May Day, when she must have been either ninety-five or six. The Blue Ribbon Oss sang and danced outside her house in Cross St. Some of us went into her front room, where she was sitting, to sing verses of the May Song to her. The Oss stuck its head into the window and her gnarled blue veined hands touched its snapper and with a deep chuckle she proudly announced 'Now I shall not be infertile'. The tradition being that any woman who was taken under the skirts of the Obby Oss would become pregnant within a year.

The organist's wife, Louie, was the great organiser of concerts which she excelled at producing, but by the time I was a choirboy she was crippled with arthritis. I did, however, take part in the last concert she organized. Some of the choirboys sang "Widdicombe Fair", acting the various characters in the song. I think she played Harry Hawke, and I remember taking yards and yards of handkerchief from her pocket to wipe the tears when we sang that verse 'Tom Pearce's old mare has not trotted home'. She was a born comedienne. Her earlier shows were much more ambitious, with fine costumes which came from the Prideaux Brune family at Prideaux Place. Humour with local associations when all the audiences knew everyone in Padstow was a great favourite in my childhood. There were two Sunday School teas in the year, one just before Christmas and the other at Whitsuntide. They were organized by the Sunday School Teachers. The Kindergarten Sunday School with Miss Doris Rouse had over one hundred children. They met each Sunday in the Church Rooms and took part in the Carol Service at Christmas and the Sunday School May Service on the first Sunday evening in May. The Girls Sunday School met in Ruthy's Lane schoolroom., with Mrs. Agnes King as its superintendent, while the Boys Sunday School was in High St. with Mrs. Tom Williams in charge.

The Church Room was full of tables laden with food and festooned with flags hung across the room. The children loved the doughnuts and jellies which formed part of the tea. At Christmas it was followed by the Prize-Giving which lasted, it seemed, hours especially if you were waiting for your prize. Much thought and preparation went into the buying of prizes suited to children of different ages. The level of noise and excitement increased as the evening progressed and it was often difficult to hear your name called out. The prizes certainly encouraged the children, and all of the Kindergarten pupils received one. The second tea was around Whitsuntide, which was the time when the church organised sports in a field off Trethillick Lane. The winners of these races received 3d or 4d each. The choirboys were paid a small amount for their services. I think it was a 1/2d a service for the Junior Choirboys and 1d for the Senior Choirboys. At the end of each quarter, on the Monday following Quarter Day, we received our money. It was exciting to receive the money I remember. One Quarter I received about four shillings, a princely sum in those days. I strove hard each Quarter to receive full attendance, which I usually did. The Church's year has a wonderful pattern, and the particular events associated with each Festival added to my interest in the church. Advent meant that Christmas was not far away

and the purple frontals and hangings were matched by the great hymns of that season. About a fortnight before Christmas the Sunday School Tea and Prize giving already described was held on a Wednesday afternoon. We obtained permission, when at Grammar School, to travel home on an earlier train so as to be at the tea which began at four o'clock.

On the Sunday before Christmas, in the evening, the Children's Carol Service was held, which took the form of a modified nine lessons and Carols with special carols by the Kindergarten, girls and boys Sunday Schools. It was at one of these Carol Services that I first read the lesson in the Parish Church. I was nervous and apprehensive but read clearly and distinctly, surprising some of the congregation. I think the passage I read was from the Book of Isaiah which began "Moreover the Lord spoke again unto Ahaz", "Ask thee a sign of the Lord Thy God" - the sign being that a virgin would conceive and bear a son. I felt great satisfaction at reading in front of a full church. The Kindergarten often sang 'Away in a Manger' or 'Little Jesus Sweetly Sleep', and the older children slightly more ambitious carols. The service ended with the Processional hymn which was always 'Once in Royal David's City'. This was an impressive sight with between one hundred and one-hundred-and- fifty children walking behind the crucifer and robed choir. The three banners which were kept in the Church were carried, the Sunday School banner by one of the Sunday School Teachers while the servers in red cassocks and cottas carried the Mothers Union banner and that of the Perseverance Guild. This guild was for Communicants set up by either the Revd. Ernest Clarabut or the Revd. Edmund Nugent. The Guild has long since ceased to exist but its banner was proudly borne aloft in the procession.

The Christmas Day services were always the same and began with a said Celebration of the Holy Communion at seven o'clock. At about half past six the bells started their Christmas peal through the darkness of Christmas morning. When I was confirmed, at the age of thirteen, my mother and I always attended this service. There was something very special about this service, The bells had a particular message of joy, I imagined they were saying 'Christ is born in Bethlehem, Christ is born in Bethlehem' as we made our way through the darkness, for dawn had not broken. The lights of the Church were already switched on when we arrived to be greeted by the sidesman with 'Happy Christmas'. The service was said, although in earlier times, when Mr. Ravenhill's health was better, a Christmas hymn was sung at both the seven o'clock and eight o'clock Communions. The crib, placed on the children's altar, was lit up and you could see from most of the church the Nativity scene. The church was decorated with flowers, often chrysanthemums, and with much greenery - holly and ivy in evidence, and also a tall Christmas tree near to the children's altar and corner. By the time the service was over, people were waiting outside for the next service, the eight o'clock Communion. The Choral Eucharist was celebrated at eleven 0' clock with Procession, carols and sermon, and often sung to the setting by Lloyd. The service ended with the carol 'O Come "All ye faithful".

On the Sunday evening after Christmas there was always Festal Evensong when the choir sang their Christmas anthem and special carols. These Carols were often from the Oxford Book of Carols with words which seemed strange to us choirboys. 'A little child there is y'born, eia, eia'. I found the mystery of that language enthralling. The beautiful language of the liturgy and the authorised Version had a very profound effect on me. I loved the Christmas story told by St. Luke in that version which we must now call the King James Version. 'And there were in the same country shepherds abiding in the fields' .. 'She brought forth her first born son and laid him in the manger because there was no room in the inn'. 'The Word was made flesh and dwelt among us and we beheld his glory, the glory as of the only begotten son full of grace and truth'. How privileged I was to know and to experience the rich cadences of that version and of the beautiful collects of the Prayer Book.

There were the lovely stories I heard choir members tell while waiting in the Choir Vestry before or after service. The one that I remember best was the well known story of Johnny Fisher, the organ blower.

Padstow Parish Church (where author was a choirboy)

All pipe organs were hand pumped until the advent of electricity and Padstow Church was no exception. The best remembered was Johnny. He was unmarried and lived with his sisters and was probably a little simple, or 'not zackly; as we Cornish say. The most famous of his exploits happened at Christmas. The hymns for the coming Christmas Carol Service did not, for some reason, include "While Shepherds", which was his favourite. He made his disappointment known to Mr. Ravenhill with words that have been remembered by Padstownians since the event. "I don't care what Carol you play I'll blow While Shepherds." Johnny was also very forgetful and, when sent shopping by his sisters, would often be absent for great periods of time. His sisters thought of a way to remedy this, so they gave him an alarm clock which was set to a particular time and its ringing would be the signal for him to return home. Johnny queued at Hicks and Capell for the groceries they required and, on this particular day the shop was very busy. At last he reached the front of the queue and was just going to give the order to Mr. Walton Hicks when the alarm rang and to the surprise of the grocer he left the shop exclaiming 'I can't stop now I must go home, as my sisters have told me to return when the alarm rings'.

There was no Watch-night service at the Parish Church when I was a choirboy although there had been in pre-war days. The Methodist Church, opposite our house in Barry's Lane, held one which followed a Social evening. After the service, Padstow Carols were sung at Cross. The bells of the Parish Church rang the Old Year out and the New Year in.

The season of Lent meant that we had an extra Evensong on Wednesday evenings at seven o'clock which was followed by a short Choir practice transferred from Thursday. We were expected to attend this service at which different clergymen preached. We had various members of the clergy from other parts of the Deanery. I soon began to notice the differences which exist in the style and content of the Sermon, often reflecting the back-ground and churchmanship of the Preacher. We preferred those whose sermons were short. Some of the clergy had very parsonic voices which reduced the choirboys to stifled giggles, while others were theatrical, and given to loud and stentorian shouting. Some were High Church and others Low. I did not fully understand, at the time, all the differences, but remember seeing a biretta for the first time and being surprised at it being taken off and on at the name of Jesus. The attendances at these sermons were much smaller than on a Sunday. On Sunday evening we had a Metrical Litany sung, the Vicar, the Revd. Philip Slocombe, knelt at the Litany Desk and sang, in his clear voice, a verse, while we responded with the next. The Litany lengthened the service and so was not favoured by many of the choir boys.

On Palm Sunday morning we received our Palm crosses and sang the hymn 'All Glory Laud and Honour' and in the evening we sang 'The Story of the Cross', which was a lengthy hymn-type meditation on the Passion of the Lord. There was much more emphasis on the Cross and Passiontide then. Good Friday was marked by the ringing of a muffled peal and the non wearing of our choir surplices, we wore only a cassock at the service. All of the surplices were washed for Easter Day and our ruffles were starched by the Misses Crane. They were two devout clergy daughters who had a Nun as a sister who often stayed with them attending the services while in Padstow. They loved cricket and I remember discussing cricket scores with them and I learnt from them many of the reasons for various parts of the ceremonial of the church.

On Good Friday afternoon we went picking primroses at Geach's Bottoms for decorating the Church on the Saturday. Huge bunches were picked, as they grew in profusion there in the sheltered valley. The church looked beautiful for Easter Day. The flowers in the sanctuary were always "Arum Lilies' which my mother disliked, as they reminded her of funerals. Every window in the church, contained floral arrangements with the predominance of daffodils, primroses and other spring flowers. There was a definite pattern to the decoration and each window was allocated to a particular person. The Sunday School children and Teacher decorated the window in the north aisle next to the Children's altar and in front of the altar, on the floor, were masses of primroses in tiny paste pot jars and in semi-circular containers, which frequently leaked and took huge numbers of primroses to fill.

Easter Day was celebrated with two early services, at seven and eight o'clock, and a Choral Eucharist with procession at eleven. This was a very long service as we sang the Te Deum at the end of the celebration. In the evening we had Festal Evensong and Procession. The altar was ablaze with candles for this service. The contrast between the bare Sanctuary of Good Friday and the decorated lighted one of Easter Day could not have been greater. "There is a Green Hill" gave way to "Ye Choir of New Jerusalem". The collection on Easter Day was given to the Vicar and the Alms bag would often contain paper money on that occasion. The Christmas Day moneys were given to the Choir fund.

The Sunday School May Festival was always held on the first Sunday in May and the month contained Ascension Day which meant that we were also expected to attend Evensong on that day. When I was confirmed we went to an early morning communion which started at a quarter-to-seven so as to allow people to make their communion before starting work. This festival is now, sadly, little observed. Whitsunday saw the church decorated in red and white. There was then a strict rule that only red and white flowers were to be placed in the church. There was always an Anthem sung at Evensong on that day. There did not seem to be so many of these as at Easter and Christmas and we usually sang 'Come Holy Ghost' by Attwood which began with the Treble singing a long section with a particularly high note (Top G) as part of it. Much time was spent at Choir practice ensuring that the note was hit correctly. The Buffs attended the Evensong Service on alternate years. They marched to the Church, with a Band at their Head. They wore the uniform of the Order, and would read the Lessons and say special prayers. The church was particularly full on this occasion, as the Buffs came from all over Mid-Cornwall. Whitsunday was then also celebrated as the Patronal Feast of St. Petroc. The sound of upward of two hundred men singing was very impressive.

BWK as a choirboy

We occasionally sang at Weddings and were paid 6d for this. Mr. Ravenhill always played 'Moonlight and Roses' while the Registers were being signed in the Vestry. The Bridal March and the Wedding March were the only pieces of music which accompanied the Bridal Procession in and out of church. If the bride was pregnant she did not wear white and so had a quiet wedding, and we never sang on those occasions. I can never remember singing at a funeral when a choirboy. The death of the Diocesan Bishop Joey Hunkin, and the death of King George VI, were marked by the playing of the Dead March in Saul at the end of the Evensong on the Sunday following their respective demises. The low notes of this solemn piece reverberated through the church in a solemn growl. Mr. Ravenhill made the great occasions of the church real through his tremendous ability as an organist.

Another memorable service which I remember was the traditional service for the Gorsedd following it taking place at Trig Troll. The blue-robed figures of the Bards had processed with dignity up to the site of the ancient barrow there. The whole event intrigued me and also thrilled me, as it was linked with the History of Cornwall. The beautiful playing of the harp, the sound of the horn summoning the people of Cornwall to the Gorsedd, the dancing of the girls with the fruits of the earth, and the singing of the hymn 'There is a land of pure delight' in Cornish' which commemorated those Bards who had died since the previous Gorsedd. I never thought that I should be made a Bard in 1987 at Antony House. I felt very proud as to a Cornishman, there can be no greater honour. The choice of my Bardic Name, Bugel Petrok (Petroc's Shepherd) linked me with my childhood in Padstow and Cove and with the Parish of St. Petroc Minor where I was Rector. Petroc sailed up the estuary of the Camel from Wales, landing first at Trebetherick and later founding the monastery at Padstow. The estuary of the Camel played an important part in his ministry.

The sight of the corn being cut in the field at Lellizzick Farm on a hot summer's day reminded me of the reapers who first saw Petroc land at Trebetherick. The warmth of the cornfield with butterflies flying just above the uncut corn and the rabbits running out of the last section of the field before it was cut is linked to the six weeks of the school summer holiday. The summers of 1947 and 1949 were both beautiful and childhood memories of days of cloudless skies, sea sparkling like a thousand jewels, the moon at night lighting up the estuary and the hours spent on Tregirls Beach were linked with the events of history which unfolded around the estuary.

The Bardic service was, I suspect, Evensong in Cornish which is traditionally sung at the time of the Gorsedd or it could have been the Concert which follows the actual ceremony. I know we practiced special anthems for this.

Made a Bard, Antony House, 1987

The first funeral I attended at Padstow Church was that of my grandfather Wells when I was 17. He died in October 1957, following a massive heart-attack and was only very ill for a week. He had strong views on what should happen at his funeral, which he wanted to be very simple. There were no flowers not even a family wreath, no music and no mourning. We entered Padstow Church in complete silence except for the Lay Reader Mr. David Griffiths reading the sentences. The coffin looked so bare and unrelieved as my mother and I walked behind it. Gran Wells did not attend the service. He also left strict instructions not to have a headstone erected as his family had quarrelled over the tombstone of his father Henry Wells. I am often saddened and amazed at the quarrels which take place following the death of a loved one. It is usually over some small possession or even about the arrangements made for the funeral.

When I was 13 I was prepared for Confirmation. The classes took place at the Nook, which was then the Vicarage for the parish of Padstow. We attended weekly and were instructed in the usual way for Confirmation. The course centered around the Creed, the Bible, the Sacraments, and the Church's Year. I was given a small Devotional book 'My Prayer Book for Men and Boys'. One of my clearest memories of the class was of the Vicar's cat walking along the keys of the piano after having its tail pulled by it's owner. I also remember being told about the old form of singing which took place in churches in the

81

Eighteenth and Nineteenth century when there was much repetition by the Musickers or Choirs. We were told that the lady choristers would sing 'O for a man, O for a man, O for a mansion in the sky'. How often do people remember humourous examples which are given to illustrate a particular part while forgetting the actual purpose of the story.

I was confirmed on All Saints Day 1953, in Padstow Church, by Bishop Wellington, the Assistant Bishop of the Diocese. The choirboys wore their choir-robes and we sat in the front row of the church. It was an important occasion and made a great impact on an impressionable adolescent. The girls and ladies all wore white dresses and veils as they did until recent years at a Confirmation. We sung the traditional hymn 'Come Holy Ghost' as the congregation knelt, and we were confirmed in pairs.

We did not receive communion at the Confirmation as is the custom today, but were expected to attend the early communion in the Parish Church at eight o'clock on the following Sunday. It was carefully explained to the candidates, in their training, how to receive Communion correctly and not to come to church on a cold winter's morning without having had a hot cup to tea. I preferred to fast before receiving Communion as was the practice of the more Catholic members of the church. The lasting impression of those early services was the peace and silence of them. The walk through the empty streets, the silence of the large church and the quiet before and after receiving the Blessed Sacrament. We were expected to prepare carefully on the Saturday night with a form of self examination and a desire to try harder to be good after receiving communion. It was thought appropriate to make at least a monthly communion. There was a real value in starting the day in this way. The first hours of the day, especially when the weather is full of promise, are very precious. The sun rising in a cloudless sky bringing new hope, the first rays shining on a still sea when the mists have dispersed slowly, or the chill of a winter's morning when the whole landscape is covered with a thick low frost, are particularly beautiful.

Soon after my Confirmation my voice began to break and I knew that my days as a choirboy were soon to end. I then became a Server. I was trained by the Head Server, Mr. Bill Tippett, who was a Ringer and Choirman. He was a tireless worker for Padstow Church at that time being also the Caretaker of the Church Rooms and in charge of the heating system which was then heated by coal. The earlier tortoise type stoves which had discoloured the pillars nearest to them had long been replaced by radiators. The heating must have been lit on Friday evenings, as the church seemed to be warm on Sundays. I served monthly at the early celebration and it was only much later that I was allowed to take part in the Choral Eucharist at eleven o'clock. I loved being a Server and walking up to the High Altar to light the candles. We always lit them ten minutes before the Service and were expected to walk with dignity and never to rush. There was a high premium placed on reverence and dignity. You always had to kneel or stand in the sanctuary, sitting or squatting during prayer was considered to be a 'Chapel posture' or even worse.

The Parish Church at Padstow was then a very formative influence on my life. I also became a Sunday School Teacher at about the age of sixteen and helped with the Boys Sunday School which met in the Althea School Room. We had Sunday School Teachers Classes each week to prepare us for the Sunday lessons. Miss Elizabeth Derry a retired teacher, was, by then, the Superintendent of that Sunday School. She was one of three spinster sisters, all of whom were devout Anglo-Catholics. Their father had been the prison doctor at Bodmin Gaol and they had been brought up at the Parish Church in Bodmin which had a definite High Church tradition. They came to the midweek communions held on all the Red-Letter Saints Days. They walked quietly into the Lady Chapel (then called the Peace Chapel, because it contained a memorial to those men lost in the two great wars) well before the service and prayed faithfully before and after the service. The Church was their life and they maintained a definite and strict rule of life. The youngest, Miss Joan Derry, cycled each Sunday to Little Petherick to attend the Sung Mass which was celebrated there with much ceremonial, including incense. Incense was then very controversial and regarded as Roman Catholic, and a sign to many that the Church was moving into Popery. There was a residual and deep-seated hatred of Rome among many people in those days. I was clear, even from my Primary School days, that I wanted to be a Teacher although from my mid-teens onwards the possibility of being ordained frequently crossed my mind. When in the Sixth Form of the Grammar School, I was sometimes asked to read a lesson at Matins or Evensong. I had a strong voice and a tendency to dramatize these readings. The art of reading aloud is today sometimes underrated. Young people find it hard to listen, as there are so many distractions in our noisy and busy world.

The Revd. Ben Clarke began the practice of giving conducted historical tours around Padstow on Tuesday evenings at eight-fifteen. These were well supported and at such a time that visitors could attend them following their evening meals. The pattern of holidays has changed for most visitors, they stayed either in a hotel or guest-house, which usually provided dinner for their guests. He decided that he would encourage and train a group of Lay Guides to assist him with this. I was delighted to be asked to be one of them. I was, by then, in the Sixth Form at Bodmin Grammar School where I was studying History as one of my 'A Level' subjects. This was my first opportunity to talk about local history and I was determined to do it well.

I studied earnestly the Guide Book which he had written about the Church, and also all other material which I knew of which related and was relevant to, the task. Padstow Church was so steeped in history and had been an important religious centre since the coming of St. Petroc with the Gospel in the sixth century. I still have the notes taken at the classes we attended before we were allowed to begin our guided tours.

The local Historian at the time was a kind and well informed man named Walton Hicks who lived in one of the large houses in Dennis Road. These large, semi-detached houses, built some time early in the century, had the most beautiful views of the Camel Estuary, especially from the first and second floors. These were the first serious developments of 'up town', Padstow. Dennis Road had once been a lane leading to Dennis Cove where one of the principal shipyards of Padstow was situated. The rope walk of the yard occupied the area near to the lane. The yard was used for much of the repair work which necessarily went on. The nature of the North Cornish coast was such that many ships were damaged in storms and needed repair.

Each Saturday morning I would visit him at about ten o' clock and stay for two hours learning from him much of the long and distinguished history of the town. He kindly loaned me his handwritten ledgers with his local history material collected throughout his life-time. I have often wondered whether he had intended to write a history of Padstow. The ledgers were written in a beautiful cursive hand, many in green ink.

All his notes were handwritten and must have taken hours and hours to patiently record. I always felt that he must have been much happier in doing this than in serving in his grocery business, Hicks and Capell, on the Market Place.

His contact with the public in the shop meant that he knew great numbers of Padstow people and could talk to them about the past, especially when his grocery shop was not too busy.

Walton travelled on the weekly bus to Truro on each Wednesday after his retirement. He caught the bus on the quay outside Mrs. Soper's fish shop which was then the principal bus stop in the town. He travelled in all weathers carrying a frail (a small bag) with his note book and lunch in. He spent the day researching the material at the Royal Institution or visiting the West Briton Headquarters to see his friend, Claude Berry, who was then Editor of that paper.

The world of the local historian opened to me on those magic Saturday mornings when I looked at these ledgers and asked myriads of questions about the Padstow of his childhood, in the late 1880's and early 1890's when Padstow was a thriving port. His measured and thoughtful responses to this eager, inquisitive teenager showed his genial good nature and his willingness to encourage a younger person develop a knowledge of the history of the town.

I had, initially, visited him to gain information about the Parish Church but as I looked at all the material he had collected my interest broadened and I began to search and collect anything related to the history of the town.

The time passed so quickly as we sat in the large sitting room of this Edwardian House. There were periods of silence while I looked and recorded information I required. The silence was only broken by the steady tick of the fine grandfather clock and by it striking the hours and half hours. I was totally oblivious of this for I had entered the world of "Padstow Past."

About halfway through the morning his wife, Mary, opened the door and brought in two cups of tea or coffee for us. If it was coffee it was milky, being made from hot milk. The tea always seemed to have tiny specks of cream floating on the top. There was always a yeast or saffron bun, a natural accompaniment of crib in those days. The mid-morning tea and repast was always called "crib" in this part of Cornwall while further west it was 'crowst'. Some of the grander people talked of elevenses which provoked Padstownians to pull faces behind their back. There was always a great dislike of any form of pretension in Padstow. A Padstownian returning from a successful career 'up country' cultivated a particularly affected voice. On one occasion he was using this 'la-de-da' voice in a shop. The shop was full of visitors but the lady behind the counter was not impressed and in front of the whole shop, was heard to exclaim 'Don't you come in here with all those airs and graces, I can mind the time when you had a big hole in the ass of your trousers'. The man was silenced.

Mary Hicks would chat with us for a brief period before returning to the kitchen where she prepared his midday meal. Walton did not care for small talk and was anxious to resume the discussion on history. The conducted tours of the church took place in June, July, August and early September. The rota of Guides meant that you had to do two tours in a season. The tour began with a general introduction to the history of the church. You always wondered how many people would make up the party to be conducted around.

I arrived just before eight o'clock, having read my notes carefully at home before setting out. My good memory meant that I would not have to look at the book too often. We were rightly told to be honest if we did not have the answer to the questions. You never knew who was in the party. I had not realised that you might have a professional Historian who had a far deeper knowledge of church architecture, or a Clergyman with a lifetime of leading the Church's worship. I made many friends on these Tuesday evenings and they were a great help to me when I had to stand up in front of a class for the first time. I put on my black cassock and waited for the first visitors to arrive. I think some of them were surprised to see a sixteen-year-old boy waiting to welcome them. The Vicar came to introduce the Guide and so helped to establish his or her authenticity.

The tour began with an outline of the history of the church from the time of the foundation of the monastery on the site by St. Petroc in the Sixth Century. After the introduction had been given the Vicar would depart, leaving you alone with the party. I was soon in full spate, information poured out as I pumped their heads full of knowledge about each of the three churches which had stood on the site. Some of the older people were initially, disappointed to find themselves being conducted by a mere lad but by the end of the evening we had established a good rapport. The hour passed quickly and often after the tour people stayed behind to ask further questions.

If the tour was at the end of the summer it was dark before you had finished and Doris Bate would arrive with her torch to lock up the church and often she would wait patiently while the last people left. She never complained but must have wanted to lock up so that she could go home.

~ PADSTOW MAY DAY ~

There was and is one day in the year which is like no other time to all Padstownians, and this is. of course, May Day. It is the Mecca which draws home many exiles to their home town. It is the day when grown men who cannot be there to celebrate it fail to hide their tears and the sense of deep home-sickness. Men in the trenches during the First World War and Sailors on the high seas during the Second War surprised their comrades by singing the haunting melody of this never-to-be-forgotten song. It is the time when the bereaved miss most keenly their loved ones. This may seem quite irrational to those who are not Padstownians but the magic of this special day bewitches those who are born in the Town and Parish.

I remember the excitement of the children at Padstow School building up in the weeks before the first of May. We always had a holiday then, but there had been times in its earlier history when the school had opened but had been virtually devoid of pupils. The pupils attending Bodmin Grammar or Wadebridge Secondary Modern Schools had the problem of stating the truth about their absence or saying that a mysterious and unknown one day sickness had afflicted them. I never went to school on May Day while attending Grammar School except for a part of a morning when preparing for 'A' level exams when in the second year sixth. The train journey on the almost empty train was like a journey into the loneliness of outer space, and the return journey seemed to be the longest ever travelled.

The preparation for May Day began some weeks before the actual day, especially if you had your own small "Oss". This was a distinct advantage, and often the envy of others. The Osses had to be in good condition to come out on May Day. The playground was full of children discussing the merits of the 'Old Oss' or the 'Peace Oss' as it was then called. The vital question asked was 'Are you Old Oss or Peace Oss'. The boys were divided in their allegiance and this was defended often with fists, in the scuffles which broke out in the playground.

There was a fierce and protective loyalty to the respective 'Osses' and there still is. Sometimes people changed their support but this was a decision of such magnitude that it could lead to a loss of a former friendship. The accident of birth usually determined which you followed. I have always followed the 'Blue Ribbon Oss', as it is now called, but have the greatest admiration for the way in which both 'Osses' and their followers keep the unique tradition alive.

The division of people into various groups was very much part of my childhood. You were either 'Church or Chapel' 'Liberal or Tory' 'Peace Oss or Old Oss'. The wearing of the political colours at election times was much more prevalent then than now. Children would sport the 'red, white and blue' rosette of the Conservative Party or the 'Red and Yellow' of the Liberal party. The red of the Labour party was a real rarity.

The Old Oss, which is the original one, is kept in the stable behind the Golden Lion from where it emerges to dance around the streets of Padstow. The Peace Oss, in my childhood days, had its stable in the Old Market with its double doors and it was from there that it made its entrance. The "Blue Ribbon Oss" now comes into view from the entrance to the Institute.

No one really knows the origin of the day but it is certainly of great antiquity. It is a fertility rite celebrating signs of new life and the death of winter. The lengthening days and the increasing warmth of the sun were so important to Prehistoric and Early Man. Although its origin is undoubtedly pagan, it is not kept up with any pagan intentions. It is the celebration of community rejoicing in all that is good about belonging and having roots within it. There is a wonderful sense of friendship, happiness, and of solidarity among those who take part. The warmth of welcome to those exiles who return home and the pride of being 'Padsta' is most marked. There is a natural joy about it which cannot be expressed in words. We grew up with certain scraps of information about its history. Tradition had it that at some time during a war with France, probably during a time between the fourteenth and early nineteenth century, Padstow was threatened with invasion by a French fleet and so the 'Obby Oss' was taken to Stepper Point, at the mouth of the estuary, where it performed the dance-thereby frightening away the French, who supposed it to be 'the Devil'. This can well be imagined as the black and grotesque creature with its fearsome mask was indeed a ferocious sight.

There were many people in Victorian times who regarded it with much suspicion and contempt and there was a serious attempt made by Thomas Tregaskis, of Sea Mills in the parish of St. Issey, to stop May Day. He was a Class Leader, Local Preacher and Revivalist who was one of the first to sign the pledge when the teetotal movement took root in Cornwall. He offered to give the inhabitants of Padstow a fat bullock for seven consecutive years if they would sink the Oss in the sea. He put up posters in the town with this offer.

*'To the Proprietors of the Hobby Horse of Padstow. This
is to give you notice that on or about the end of this month
I shall offer you the Bullock according to promise, it is for
you to consult against that time, whether you will give up your
vain practice of the Hobby, for the rational amusement of
eating Roast Beef. Padstow, April 10th 1845. Thomas Tregaskis'.*

The reply, which was posted on another placard in the town, rejected this offer and stated with passion that 'The bones of every Padstow Boy are fired by the Hobby Horse. As soon as a child is able to lisp its parent's name it will chant the glorious strains of our ancient Festival Song and will usher in May's first merry morn with 'The Summer and the Summer and May O'.

'And shall we allow aliens and strangers to usurp our pleasures and rob us of our birthright, that we have inherited from Mother to Daughter, from Father to Son, No, we will not'..

From the great encouragement we have received from every grade of society in town we are determined the entertainments of this year shall greatly surpass preceding ones.

Given under the Great Seal of The Hobby Horse Fraternity Drew, Printer and Binder Bodmin'.

In my childhood the actual celebration began at midnight, when the clock of the Parish Church struck the first stroke of that bewitching hour. There was no singing in the streets before that time. In my early teens, when I was allowed to go 'Night Singing' as it is called, the crowd would gather outside the Golden Lion and wait, with growing excitement, for the hour to come. In those days the street lights went out just before midnight, so the singing began in almost total darkness except for the lights of the pub and of the surrounding houses. The babble of excited chatter stopped as the clock struck, and the song began.

*'Unite and unite and let us all unite,
For summer is acome unto today,
And whether we are going we will all unite,
In the merry morning of May."*

At one of the upstairs windows of the Golden Lion were to be seen the publican Mrs. Maud Couch and her daughter, Winnie.

*" Arise up Mrs. Couch and gold be your ring,
For summer is acome unto day,
And give to us a cup of ale and the merrier we shall sing,
In the merry morning of May."*

The strong voices sang this verse to her. Many of these fine singers of my youth are now dead, but the night singing is still of a very high standard, After singing two or three more verses, the final one began.

*" Now we fare you well, and we bid you all good cheer,
For summer is acome unto day,
We'll call once more unto your house before another year,
In the merry morning of May."*

We moved up Church Lane to sing to Doreen Pengelly and her family at their home. This good-natured and kind Padstownian always had a house full for May Day. The stars filled the sky if the weather was clear and there was often a decided nip in the air, as often at the beginning of May we seem to have a rather cold spell. No one ever said they were cold because they were warm inside, happy to sing to the older Padstownians before going 'Up-town' to complete the night singing. The route was pretty well charted, and as the first verse of the Night Song was struck up a light would be seen at the bedroom window and sometimes it would be opened and a happy face would appear. It was a great privilege to receive a visit from the night-singers.

One of the most difficult parts of the route was the steep descent from Oak Terrace through the gardens and steps into Duke Street. The party always sang to Mr. and Mrs Edgar Williams and Johnny Rosevear, who lived there. The Williamses were the Newsagents in the Market Square for many years. Some of the party carried torches and, like a gigantic glow worm with its little lights the procession made its slow and tortuous way down the hazardous route. Voices could be heard 'Mind the step'. 'Watch out there's dog's mess there!' 'Look out, or you will be in the bushes; 'I nearly fell, there's a pile of loose stones there.' If it was a moonlit night you could see the whole of the estuary from Padstow Quay to Rock and up the river to Gentle Jane and Camel Quarry and watch the shadows ever changing on the water. This added to the magic of the night.

Sometimes, as they sang to the elderly, the singers knew they would not be singing next year to the person as they were terminally ill. The voices seemed gentler and full of concern, it was as if there was a shared knowledge and understanding of the situation. The darkness often hid tears on these occasions. You could not live in this tight-knit community without having a real and lasting bond with your fellow townsfolk.

At the bottom of the steps from Oak Terrace I would return home to Barry's Lane, as it was by now about one thirty in the morning, while the singers continued well into the night. It was the early hours of the morning before they had completed the whole route.

The morning of May Day was soon upon me for I could only sleep fitfully such was the level of my excitement. You could hear the children 'Osses' dancing in the streets well before eight o'clock. The early morning dancing of the children had a particular freshness. The streets were bedecked with all kinds of flags and by the telegraph poles and at the corner of the streets were the branches of sycamore and other green boughs which had been picked in the early hours, at about six o'clock, and placed in these strategic positions.

I rushed down to see the finishing touches being made to the beautiful May Pole in Broad Street. Walter Chapman, with his great artistic gifts, had spent hours preparing, with a group of others, the hoops and the decorations which made it look superb. Around the base of the May Pole were the bunches of spring flowers particularly cowslips, bluebells and lilies-of-the valley, I sported my own button hole of similar flowers as I rushed frantically around the town hoping to see the childrens' 'Osses.'

The gusto of the singing, the rhythmic banging of the drums, and the sound of an occasional accordian told of the approach of one of the Osses. Soon they came in sight, visitors looked with a certain degree of amusement at the totally uninhibited dancing of the children with the Oss.

All of the Osses are basically the same, although the childrens' one, of course, smaller. The oss is a large hoop, covered with black material hanging down at each side in a skirt-like formation. In the middle of the top of the material is a round hole into which the person who carries the Oss places his head. A ferocious, conical mask is then tied over his head. The Oss has snappers at the front and a small tail of the back. It is very hard work carrying it and so frequently changes are necessary if the vigorous dancing is to continue. The Oss is led, or 'teased', by the Teaser, who is a man or woman carrying a club with a design on it. Although I have never carried the Oss, I have had the privilege of being the Teaser.

The 'Peace Oss' or 'Blue Ribbon Oss' makes its appearance first. In my youth it came out at10.30am but now it emerges at 10.00am. The Market Square or Place is jammed full of people by the time it appears. Padstownians jostle for position so that they can be at the front of the crowd. The musicians appear first and then, with a mighty rush, the Oss rushes forth and begins its vigorous and invigorating dance. The singing is always at its best in the morning when everything is fresh. Crowds were much smaller in former times and it was always much easier for the Oss to dance. At one time when a woman was caught by the oss and taken under its skirts her face was blacked. This was all part of the original fertility rite. Attractive young woman have always been a target for the 'Oss'! Many younger visitors have been somewhat terrified by it and I can remember the screams of many a young woman as it has caught her.

The Old Oss sallies forth from its stables at the Golden Lion at 11.00am, this, too is an earlier time than in the past when it began its dance at 11.30am. The streets around the Golden Lion are completely filled by the crowds awaiting the moment of its appearance. The Osses dance throughout the day and well into the evening with only short breaks for lunch and tea. All the public houses of the town are filled to overflowing and remain open all day.

One of the chief joys of this very special day is meeting up with old friends who have made the journey home from all over the country, indeed all over the world, just to be home in Padstow. It is as if conversations are resumed where they were left off, twelve months or, even several years, before. Sadly, as each year passes some exiled Padstownians return home no more as age or death catches up with them. There is always a pathos in the joy of the May Day.

There have been, for many years, stalls selling all kinds of objects and cheap-jacks pedalling their wares. At one time they were on the actual quayside. Stalls, or "stannings" as they used to be called, came to Padstow on a number of occasions in the year. Some of the best loved stalls sold sweets, clidgy or toffee apples in former years. They always seemed to have good trade although there must have been lean years when money was tight. I am reminded of that when I hear the lovely expression "stick to your stanning even if you don't sell an happorth"! This determined, stubborn streak is very much part of our Cornish make up. On May Day we Padstownians refuse to budge from the front places in the crowds where we rightly belong, for May Day is our day.

The most emotional part of the day is the Farewell, which is sung before the Osses finally are put to rest for another year. This part of the day is relatively modern in origin. It was introduced by Mr. Bill Thomas, who dressed up as a lady on May Day and was a prominent member of the 'Peace Oss'. It was first sung just after the end of the First World War.

The words have their origin in a typical Victorian ballad;

> " One parting kiss I give thee
> I cannot bear to leave thee
> I go where duty calls me
> I go what'er befalls me
> Farewell, farewell my own true love
> Farewell, farewell, my own true love."

As the song is sung, the whole atmosphere is charged with a deep emotion. Many of the 'Mayers' are in tears, for this marks the end of Padstow special day for another year. In recent years this music is often played at the end of the funeral of a Padstownian as the cortege leaves the Parish Church or Methodist Church.

It is undoubtedly very sentimental and touches the highly emotional Cornish Celtic nature deeply.

After a day of constant singing and dancing I was always exhausted and often was in danger of losing my voice. When I was Headmaster of St. Issey School there was always an expectation that children would need to be particularly quiet on the day after May Day and that I would not be able to raise my voice to an erring pupil.

Much humour has always been made of my participation in the May Day celebrations. When the 'Si Quis' was going to be read at Padstow Church before my ordination could take place some of my fellow ordinards threatened to object and state that I had taken part in May Day which was originally a fertility rite.

I well remember a sermon preached by the then Curate, Revd. Malcolm Byrom, now the Vicar of the Kenwyn, which had its text 'Oss Oss, Wee Oss' which is, of course, the cry that is periodically shouted during the dancing. This cry, whose origin is somewhat of a mystery, has obvious links to the whinny of a horse. He used this text to show that there was a need for the Church to exhibit the same unity of purpose and joy that is exhibited in Padstow on May Day.

In the Coronation year of 1937 when King George VI was crowned, a party of townswomen, including that great and well loved character Rosie Walker (Sorensen), brought out their own Oss. Rosie was one of the most politically conscious people I knew in my childhood. She was a fervent Liberal and well known at the political meetings which then took place in the old Public Rooms. She had a sharp mind and a ready answer.

One of the best remembered incidents was when, with a party of Padstow Liberals, she walked to St. Merryn to attend a Conservative pre-election meeting. The hall at St. Merryn was crowded, and she and her party sat themselves in the front rows of the hall. The then Chairman of the conservatives had, not long before, been involved in a court case where he had been accused of watering the milk he sold to customers. He saw, with apprehension, the arrival of the Padstow contingent, who had obviously come to heckle and ask awkward questions of the Candidate. There was always a period of waiting before the Candidate, who had a tight schedule, arrived, and the Chairman had to keep the 'pot boiling' until he came. He inquired, rather injudiciously, of the newly arrived political opponents "Why have you Padstow Liberals come to St. Merryn?" The retort was instant as Rosie, a large lady, with a huge red and yellow rosette, silenced him by stating, 'we have come to see the cow with the iron-tail".

On another occasion Rosie was tusslling with the Conservative MP for North Cornwall, 1924-29, who was one of the Williams family of Werrington. It was a friendly exchange and she probably had the best of the argument. After the meeting was over he graciously came over to her mother, Fanny Truman, who was sitting on the Long Lugger remarking that Rosie had a wonderful repartee. 'Oh es, she's a handsome cook', her proud mother commented.

One of the strongest men ever to carry the Old Oss was William Henry Baker (1856-1924), who lived next door to the Kinsman family at Hawkers Cove. My aunts remember him chasing a young woman the length of the North Quay to catch her. He even jumped the churchyard wall while carrying the Oss. This powerful man was the Coxswain of the Arab Lifeboat.

Padstow May Day

89

~ BODMIN GRAMMAR SCHOOL ~

In September1951 I began seven happy years attending the local Grammar School in Bodmin. The school began as a private school and was then known as 'Harleigh'. In 1902, with the passing of the Education Act, it became known as Bodmin County School and was open to non-paying pupils. Those wishing to obtain these free places had to pass the Scholarship. This was a clear step forward but many of the poorer families could not afford the train fares and the uniform which was expected to be worn. In 1944 the great Butler Education Act abolished the private element in the school. All pupils attending it had to pass the Scholarship, later to become the 'Eleven-plus.' The children were all given a free season-ticket to travel on the train and those who were less well off had grants towards their school uniform. The competition for places at the school became very keen. Many parents regarded a Grammar School education as a status symbol. There can be no doubt that the Grammar School system allowed children of working class parents an opportunity to make their way into jobs which had been previously open only to the middle classes. In Cornwall about twenty-five per cent of pupils were given a Grammar School education. The remaining seventy-five per cent remained at the local school, which was still an all-age one. This was the case in Padstow until 1957 when Wadebridge Secondary Modern, now Wadebridge Comprehensive School opened.

Some weeks before the beginning of the term the school uniform list was sent to the parents, and all the necessary clothes were bought including School cap, then so faithfully worn but often lost in horse-play on the school train or from the school cloakroom. Grey shirts with the black and red school tie, blazer, and short grey trousers for the younger boys formed part of the uniform. Most boys wore shorts until about the age of thirteen. Plimsolls and P.E. shorts for use in the gymnasium. There were no showers at the school then. You had to change for P.E. in the Boys cloakroom. The first morning at a new school is always a daunting experience for an eleven-year-old. One of the older boys, Michael Nicholson, called for me and, in the company of other Padstow boys, we walked to the station to catch the 8.10am train. I was dressed in school uniform with my satchel strapped on my back. I had my fountain pen, for no biros were used, my geometry set with protractor, compass, set square, rubber and pencil, all in the satchel. All my clothing had been faithfully labelled with Cash name tapes so that the forgetful boy could not lose them. The loss of clothes or other items would have been costly. My mother was working in the breadshop of Eustaces in Padstow to earn a relatively small wage, although, even by then she had indifferent health, she was prepared to work hard so that I could have the right education.

The platform at Padstow Station was full of pupils by the time we arrived. There were also many local people, who worked in Wadebridge or Bodmin, on their way to work waiting for the train. It was a general train although sections were reserved for the Grammar School children. Passengers desiring a quiet and uneventful trip to work kept well clear of the noisy pupils.

The carriages, when I first travelled to school, often did not have corridors and were old Southern Railway rolling-stock. Each carriage had, in theory, a prefect who was responsible for the behaviour of the children in it.

The journey to Bodmin General or 'Great Western' Station, as it was referred to, was always an eventful one. Much of the time was spent with certain of the pupils catching up with their homework which had not been done on the previous evening. Some of the more adventurous pupils would climb from carriage to carriage along the board at the side of the train. I have even seen the most dare-devil of the boys climb on the top of the train while it was in motion. Shoes and socks, and even underclothes, were passed from carriage window to carriage window. One poor boy lost his trousers and had to walk to school with his mack on to hide this loss. They were, I believe, returned to him before school started. Some travelled in the old fashioned rack where the luggage was supposed to be.

The train took about three quarters of an hour to travel via Wadebridge, Grogley Halt, Nanstallon Halt and Boscarne Junction to its destination. The last part of the journey from Boscarne necessitated the train pulling up a relatively steep gradient and on icy mornings this often caused the train to come to a sudden halt to the massive cheers of the children on the train! In very wet periods the railway line between Wadebridge and Boscarne would be flooded.

The Grammar School was only about 200 metres from the station so there was not a great walk. Before 1948, when British Railways took over the whole of the network, the pupils had to walk from Bodmin Southern Station which was at least a mile from the school. On the first day at school we were given the Timetable for the week. Most of the lessons were taken in the first form room and the teachers moved around the school from classroom to classroom. The school operated with two parallel forms, East and West, and there was no form of streaming. In the fourth and fifth year subjects were setted into those taking the GCE examination and non-examination groups.

Each morning we had a school Assembly for the whole school in the Hall with the service conducted by the Headteacher, Mr. C. V. Marks. He was a good and kind man who was somewhat lame. The Service followed the same pattern each day, with a hymn from the Songs of Praise hymnbook, a reading from the Bible, which was a shortened version with selected readings, the Lord's Prayer, usually sung, and other prayers, followed by the notices. The Teachers, in their gowns, sat on the platform at the front of the hall. Some teachers attended assembly regularly while others rarely came. I do not remember a clergyman of any denomination taking part in the assembly. The lessons were read on a rota basis with a different form providing the Readers each week. The hymns were often accompanied by one of the senior pupils on the piano. A much wider variety was sung than at Primary School. At the beginning of each term we dutifully sung 'Lord Behold Us with Thy Blessing' and at the end 'Lord Dismiss us with thy Blessing'. This was sung with much greater vigour. I can remember as a sixth-former, reading that most beautiful passage from the thirteenth chapter of St. Paul's first letter to the Corinthians 'Though I speak with the tongues of men and of angels and have not Charity'.

At break time on the first day, the time honoured custom of ducking the boy's head in a basin of water took place. This was far less barbaric than many other initiation customs which other schools used. There was a little bullying in the school but it was not encouraged as the Head Teacher ran a very humane establishment. Some of the new pupils were forced by older boys to sing in the playground for the first few days.

We were issued with our sets of text books for the various subjects. There was no question then of having to buy them. At the front of each book was a label where you wrote your name with the condition of the book on a five point scale A-E, the idea being that you were responsible for it and looked after it. We each had our own desk which was deep enough to contain all of the books, both text and exercise books. When an exercise book was full the teacher signed it and you collected a new one from the office where the school secretary worked.

The punishment system was a simple one. You were given a punishment book which was used when you were given work to do in detention. A detention was given for a fairly serious offence, while disorder marks were given for lesser misdemeanours. Three disorder marks meant a detention. The Detention class took place after school on a particular evening of the week until about five o'clock which meant that you had to catch a later train. The use of the cane was rare. The Headteacher had his office at the end of the school near to the foot of the stairs to the first floor of the main building. The hardened offender would have to wait in the corridor outside his office, where the punishment was carried out. There was talk of one or two senior pupils being expelled, but I cannot remember this happening while I was there. There were also whispers about senior girls being pregnant and having to leave school while the baby was born but there was no evidence of this either. I had left school before the permissive sixties were in full swing.

Each term you received a school report which contained two gradings. The first on a five point scale, A - E with pluses and minuses added was for attainment and the second for effort, either Good, Satisfactory or Unsatisfactory with a plus or minus if required, to refine the assessment. Only the top three places in the form were made public, although similar placing in subjects received recognition.

The school sought to encourage you to improve your own performance rather than to compare it with others. There was a certain amount of speculation and interest about the position at the top of the form. You were expected to return the report at the end of the holiday signed by a parent. All reports were sent home in sealed brown envelopes. Many of them were steamed opened and re-sealed during the train journey. My mother allowed me to look at mine, so there was no surreptitious opening and re- sealing necessary. My reports were very good at the beginning of my grammar school life, but went through a less satisfactory period in the middle years. The sixth form allowed me to blossom again. I loved my two years there, they were two of the happiest years of my life. There was no doubt that the strength of my academic life lay in the Arts subjects, although not in Art itself which was probably my poorest.

By the time I reached the Sixth Form it was clear that I was best at History, English and Geography which I studied for A level'. Although I managed seven 0 level subjects and three 'A' levels I certainly did not realise my potential as my work was often rather untidy and I worked hard at only the subjects which I enjoyed. The Sixth Form saw me blossom and I enjoyed all three of the courses taken. I was very fortunate to have Miss Olive Spear as my Geography teacher, for she set very high standards and expected the best of you. She was a rigid disciplinarian to the younger pupils. The sixth former knew her to be concerned for them and prepared to take much time to see that they succeeded in their exams. History was taught me by three masters. Mr. Todd, who also taught me Scripture, took the lower school. He was a very intelligent man but he had difficulty in keeping order. His lessons were frequently interrupted by the throwing of pencils, rubbers and even raucous laughter. This was sad as I liked him and did well in the subjects. Mr. Dick Roberts took the 'O level' History group. He was also the P.E. and Games teacher. He was universally liked and respected, with the ability to command respect without even raising his voice. He prepared model answers for the usual questions which occurred in the History papers. These history notes were used by generations of pupils at the school.

I did not enjoy the P.E. lessons in the Gymnasium as I have very small hands and a poor grip. I much preferred the Cricket lessons in the summer or playing tennis on the grass tennis courts at the school. Mr. Wilfred Webster was the Latin master, and in alternate years he took the A level, History group. He was a good natured 'Yorkshireman' who had been gassed during the First World War and so periodically suffered certain internal problems.

One of the greatest characters was the Chemistry Master Mr. F. A. Nurse, who bore the nickname 'Fanny'. He was a bachelor with a tremendous sense of humour and a great actor.

Chemistry lessons in the laboratory were often very humourous as he cracked jokes, often about the work of the pupils. He produced many of the school plays which were presented. He always wore a bow tie and was, I believe, a preacher in the Congregational Church at Bodmin. The School Plays were produced and took place in the Public Rooms at Bodmin, where, each year, the School Speech Day was held.

Speech Day was not a popular occasion. The whole school attended this event which usually took place towards the end of the Spring Term. The Public Rooms were full and it became very stuffy and close on occasions. We were marched, in twos, from the school, down St. Nicholas St, to the hall. The proceedings followed a set pattern and various prizes were presented. There were the prizes for the first three in each form and prizes for 'O' Level results and 'A' level. I believe that candidates with five or more 'O' Levels and three 'A' levels received prizes. Subject awards were given for the best 'A' level result in that field. Various local dignitaries made speeches, including the then Mayor of Bodmin, and there was always someone of note to present the prizes and give the main speech. On one occasion the prizes were presented by Prince Chula of Siam, who lived at Tredethy. The platform was flanked by the Governors of the School, only Grammar and Secondary Modern Schools had governors then. Primary Schools had Managers.

The theme of the Address by the guest who gave the prizes was usually predictable - it rang something like this 'It is good to be here today sharing in the Annual Speech and Prize Giving. I would like to congratulate those who have been awarded prizes and certificates, of course, not all of you can do this but I am sure that all of you can give of your best to the school and be proud of belonging to such a happy and successful school'. The Chairman of the School Governors then thanked the Speaker, and the Staff for their hard work during the past academic year. It may seem strange to many today but we were proud of the school and of its achievement for there was always a great sense of belonging among the pupils. We knew all the staff and most of the pupils, who numbered between 300 and 400.

There was very keen competition between the three houses into which all pupils were placed on arrival. I was placed in St. Petroc's House and wore a yellow badge and, when I became a Prefect, a yellow Prefects badge. Other pupils belonged to Harleigh, which had red as its colour, or Pentire, which sported blue badges. The keenest competition was always in evidence when the School held its annual Sports Day with the usual variety of track and field events. There were House matches in cricket, football, netball, hockey and tennis. Various members of staff were allocated to different houses.

A number of interesting events are firmly placed in my mind. One of the most bizarre was of standing outside the Assize Court and seeing Miles Gifford, who was convicted of murder, leave the Courtroom. As part of our history course we were taken to see a Civil case at the Quarter Sessions. We sat on the hard benches in the old Court-room and observed, at first hand, the English legal system.

The Annual Inter-Grammar-School sports were held each year and I can remember us going to St. Austell Grammar School, then divided into a boys and girls school for this event. The most distinctive memory is of the strong smell coming from the premises of St. Austell Brewery which was situated next to the school.

We had Christmas parties each year and, when in the Sixth Form, a number of after-school socials. This was the era of Rock and Roll, and Bill Haley and the Comets. The Sixth Form was then situated in a new classroom outside the main building. There was a record player which was used during the dinner time and even at break time. The School allowed the Sixth Form a reasonable amount of freedom, which was good.

We much enjoyed the Carol Singing, which took place annually around the streets of Bodmin collecting for the Sunshine Homes for Blind Babies. I believe we went on two evenings, covering much of the town. We sang the traditional carols and also the French Carol 'Un flambeau Jeanette, Isabella.' It was on one of these nights that I fell down the steps in the grounds of the Roman Catholic Abbey, and had to have my ankle strapped up for a month as the ligaments were badly torn.

There was one very sad event which happened while I was in the First Year Sixth. On the day before the Upper Sixth started their A-levels in 1957, one of the pupils who was due to sit these exams was drowned in Dunmere Pool. The whole school was deeply shocked at Alan Vickery's death for he was a clever and gifted pupil with a brilliant career before him. The Head Teacher had the unenviable task of telling the school the next morning. We sang the hymn 'Lord Thy Word Abideth':

"Word of mercy, giving,
Succour to the living,
Lord of life, supplying
Comfort to the dying."

What did we all make of this? For many it was the first experience of the death of a contemporary. The whole school was stunned, tears flowed freely, many of his friends were deeply shocked and not in a condition to begin their A-level exams. The Tragedy was bitter for his parents, for he was an only son. Many of the pupils asked the perennial question "Why?" The teachers were in the background giving support in a restrained and sensible way. The funeral took place in the huge Parish Church at Bodmin where he had been a Server. We all attended, dressed in dark clothes with black ties. This was the first funeral I attended. This was soon followed by the funeral of my maternal grandfather, James Wells, who died in October 1957 following a massive heart attack. He lived for a week after this and was confused and disorientated. The funeral took place at Padstow Parish Church and was a very simple affair. He had very decided views on what should happen at this service. He had clearly stated there would be no flowers, not even family flowers, no mourning so there were no black ties or dark suits, no headstone in the cemetery so all that commemorated his and Gran Wells graves was a mound of earth.

His views on this, as on every other issue, were adamant. There had been a tremendous family row after the funeral of his father and the family had been split asunder by this. Great grandfather Wells' headstone in the City of London cemetery showed evidence of this. Although Gran and Grandad Wells had looked after him his headstone mentioned only certain of his children and Grandad Wells was not among them.

There were no hymns at the service, not even organ music before and after the short, said, funeral service. There was only the sound of the footsteps of the Bearers and the small group of mourners following the coffin on the bier. I walked with my mother, as Gran Wells did not attend, this being Grandad's wish. I distinctively remember the salute of the town's policeman as the cortege passed him as he was on the beat at the bottom of Barry's Lane and one or two mens' hats raised as a mark of Respect as we made our way slowly to the Parish Church.

During my years at Bodmin I became a keen tennis player and greatly enjoyed playing, both on the grass tennis court behind the sixth form block and on the hard courts at the Car Park in Padstow. Tennis became part of my young life and I became the Captain of the Second Six at Culham College of Education where I trained as a teacher.

My love of Literature greatly developed in the sixth form at Bodmin. The good-natured and sensitive approach to teaching English engendered by Sam Lucas, Head of the English Department, must have aided and stimulated this interest. The Prologue to the Canterbury Tales by Chaucer formed part of the English Literature 'O' level course but it was tales like the Millers Tale which aroused the greater interest of the pupils. I am sure that the collective works of Geoffrey Chaucer were well read even by those who had no great literary interests. This was about the time when Penguin published a paper back edition of his works. This much thumbed volume opened at the Millers' Tale as this was the most read of all his tales. I can also remember reading 'Moll Flanders', which contained some descriptions which were then considered a little racy, and by us a sign of being grown up and able to understand the descriptions. All of this was prior to the publication of Lady Chatterley's Lover which took place while I was studying to be a teacher. It was said that the local book shop in Abingdon, near to Culham College of Education, sold out and had to re-order as the students bought all the copies.

First year sixth form, Bodmin Grammar School. Author 2nd from left, front row

There were the plays of Shakespeare studied both at 'O' and 'A' Level. I am very grateful that I learnt by heart some of the great passages from these plays. We studied "Midsummer Night's Dream" and I believe that the school performed this on one occasion in the Public Rooms at Bodmin. "The Merchant of Venice" and "The Winters Tale" were two of the plays which formed part of the A-level course. I was also introduced to a number of Twentieth Century Poets, as we studied them. I loved, and still love, the poems of T. S. Eliot and C. Day Lewis. The sombre mood and element of doubt contained in them was reflected in my own questioning of my adolescent faith which had accepted without question the literal truth of the Bible and Creeds which I heard Sunday by Sunday at Church. There was a period during the sixth form when I virtually lost my faith although I still attended church faithfully. The two years at Culham College of Education, where I studied Divinity and came to terms with modern biblical scholarship and the need to present the Christian faith intelligently, gave me a more mature and reflective faith. My faith has always had within it a deep sense of questioning and an acknowledgement that we cannot know in this life all that we would like to know about God.

~ NUMBER FOUR IS NO MORE ~

Number Four Hawkers Cove was the hub of a network of family contacts. It was always 'Home' to the family until a tragic day in November 1975. A day that for all of us marked the end of an era. It was a Friday, but not the thirteenth. I was at St. Issey School where I had already been Head Teacher for nine years. Morning school was just over and I was in

my study checking dinner registers with Eileen Gool, who was the secretary there. Eileen was a Nugent before her marriage, and had been born at Number Six Pilot Houses. The Nugents and Kinsmans have always been great friends. My grandmother always helped Mrs. Nugent whenever she had a baby. No doubt she had taken in some of her delicious cooking to help with their large family at those times. Eileen and her husband, Eric, are still great friends of mine. Her delicious yeast buns are a particular favourite and I am given one whenever I call on them in their bungalow in School Hill. The telephone rang. It was a call from Cove from Alice England, the immediate neighbour to my Aunt. She was obviously agitated and distressed. Aunty Kath wanted me to come at once as there had been a fire at Number Four. I replied that I would be there as quickly as possible. I had hardly put the phone down when there was another call, this time from my Mother, for by now the news had reached her. She wanted to go to Cove to see if she could help. I ran to my car which was parked each day in front of the Georgian Vicarage at St. Issey which was later to become my home. At great speed I drove to the top of Place Hill where I had arranged to pick up my mother and take her to Cove. At this time we little realised the full extent of the damage. We were soon at Lellizzick Farm, where we could see smoke blowing across the estuary from Cove. It was obviously more than a chimney fire. As we began the descent of the hill it was clear that it was a very serious fire. At the foot of the hill there were three fire engines. The house appeared to be seriously damaged, smoke was still billowing from the burning building.

There was an eerie silence about the estuary. The weather was remarkably still for November. The estuary looked as beautiful as ever. It was as if it was paying a farewell tribute to all those happy memories we had of this idyllic place.

I raced on ahead of my mother to the end of the cement. The scene set out before me was like a battle-field. There were no human casualties but the firemen, many with their breathing apparatus, were working with great skill to bring the fire under control. The masks were essential because of the intensity of the smoke. At the bottom of the garden opposite the back door were pieces of charred furniture, many of them barely recognisable.

Before I had a closer look at the house, my mother and I went into Alice England's house. It was not like the happier times when I had called there for Brian England, one of my childhood friends, or when I had passed the ever-open back door and smelt the delicious aroma of fish frying in Alice's kitchen.

The call had a finality about it. Aunty Kath, looking very badly shaken was sitting on the settee. She found it difficult to speak but kept on repeating "I was only upstairs for a few minutes". Gradually the sequence of events began to unfold. She had started to prepare her dinner and had placed some chips in a frying pan on the top of the electric stove. She had left the pan on the stove while she went upstairs to finish packing, as she was going to stay with her sister, Lena, and brother-in-law, Donald for the winter including the Christmas period. Each winter she went to one of her sisters or to her brother to stay and to spend Christmas with them. In the latter years of Gran's life this had been the pattern. No longer did they come to Cove during Christmas but Gran and Aunty Kath visited them in rotation. She must have stayed longer than she had imagined upstairs. It was the smell of the smoke which caused her to return downstairs to the kitchen. By that time the kitchen was a raging inferno of flames, smoke was filling the tiny room. She made an immediate exit and was lucky to escape without serious injury. The fire intensified almost immediately when one of the gas cylinders which she kept exploded. The sound of the explosion was heard by people up to a mile away. If the wind had been strong, and the day not remarkably calm for November, the whole of the Pilot Row would have been damaged by fire. Thankfully, it was limited to one house. The walls of the next door house were quite warm and this made us realise how near it came to spreading to the other properties. We sent for the Doctor, as we realised Aunty Kath had experienced a great shock. Her health was not good as she had a heart condition and also a mild form of diabetes. The Doctor came promptly and assured us that she was only badly shaken. The long term effect on her health and happiness were much more serious.

By this time the fire was fully under control and it was safe for me to enter the house. For the first time in my life I dreaded this. I finally plucked up courage and went to survey the damage. The firemen had been magnificent, limiting the fire to this one house, but the scene which awaited me is clearly etched on my mind today as it was on that fateful day in November,1975.

The kitchen was totally gutted by fire. It was a blackened shell. Nothing remained of the furniture and familiar objects which I had known since childhood. Jabez and Claude's portraits were no more. They no longer surveyed all the happenings in this, once busy and loved kitchen. It was as if they had never existed. I realised how transitory our possessions are, and how valuable is the gift of memory.

It was in the front room that the loss of the home hit me hardest. The effect of the fire was great here too, but there were vestiges remaining of charred furniture. Scattered on the floor among the ash and remains were half-burnt family photos. Most of Gran's family photographs she loved and cherished had been destroyed. The smell of the fire had been acid and choking. There was a stench of charred embers. My eyes began to fill with moisture. Was it the effects of the smoke or the deep emotion of the moment?

If I am honest, it was mostly the latter. This room with all its associations and memories, would never be the same again. All the moments of joy and happiness, all those dramas and traumas which were played out here were over.

There was an icy, uncanny presence even though heat from the fire remained. There were a few recognisable photos left but it was those which were partly burnt which evoked the deepest anguish. There was the photo of my Father, barely recognisable in his Naval uniform, there were partly destroyed photos of her grandchildren, which she especially valued, covered with soot or burnt at the edges. The clock on the wall was still hanging there but it had stopped when the effect of the heat had reached it. It could remain for ever at that time, I thought. The moment when the Family Home died.

There was no doubt that this marked the end of an Era. It was more than the end of the family home, sad and hurtful though that was. There would be no Kinsmans at Number Four Hawkers Cove for the first time for sixty-five years. The old piano on Sunday nights would no longer ease the hurts of life. The lovely Cornish teas, eaten from the large gate-legged table would cease. The wide network of family and friends who had loved this house where friendship, generosity, and the warmth of human love were found in such large measure, would be no more.

To me this event symbolises the end of a style of life which had been largely unchanged for generations.

Life was very much centred around the home and the extended family. It had been hard, for there were no labour-saving devices which the hard-pressed mother of a large family could use. She was wedded to her home and family, while her husband was the Provider of the family finance, often working long hours for little reward. The making of music, and the playing of simple games, had given way to the television and stereo and ever-increasing demands for expensive toys. The joy of seeing the family well-fed on home-made Cornish fare had been replaced by 'boughten traad' in abundance. The walk to the toilet on the edge of the cliff would be replaced by indoor sanitation when the house was rebuilt.

The Community would soon disappear from Hawkers Cove. The Lifeboat had already been re-positioned at Trevose Head, because there was no longer a channel on this side of the estuary at all tides. The French Crabbers came no more. The Church had already suffered the same fate as the house. Today the beauty of the Estuary remains unclothed and enriched by the personalities who once lived here. Only one of the Pilot houses is lived in for all of the year, the others are holiday cottages. Aunty Kath survived the fire but in many ways she died with the house. It was only just under nine months later that I was conducting her Committal at Penmount Crematorium following her funeral service at Padstow Church.

"Forasmuch as it pleased Almighty God, of his great mercy, to take unto himself the soul of our dear sister, Lottie Kathleen Elsie here departed, we therefore commit her body to be consumed by fire."